DB

Cross Stitch Greeting Cards

Cross Stitch
Greeting Cards

David & Charles

A DAVID & CHARLES BOOK

First published in the UK in 2002
First paperback edition 2004

Designs Copyright: Julie Cook © pages 55*, 58*, 76*, 79, 81
Sue Cook © pages 11*, 14, 17, 28, 30*, 38, 45, 71*, 93*
Claire Crompton © pages 12*, 24, 27*, 35, 36, 39*, 46*, 49*, 60, 75*, 89*, 90, 92, 94
Maria Diaz © pages 13*, 19*, 24, 29*, 31, 34, 57, 61*, 74, 80*, 82, 87, 92
Sam Hawkins © pages 10, 11, 37, 62*, 63, 68, 69*, 70*
Susan Penny © pages 27, 33, 40, 47*, 48, 50*, 71, 72, 77, 78
Helen Philipps © pages 16, 18*, 44*, 56, 59, 64, 73, 96*
Mari Richards © pages 20, 30, 32, 39, 61, 90
Lesley Teare © pages 12, 15*, 20, 25, 26*, 32*, 45*, 54*, 60*, 77, 91* , 94
Anne Wilson © pages 46, 86*, 88, 95*
Where two charts appear on one page, turn to that page to identify the designer of each.
Designs marked with an * include a matching tag.
Photography, text and layout Copyright © David & Charles 2002, 2004

Distributed in North America
by F&W Publications, Inc.
4700 East Galbraith Road
Cincinnati, OH 45236
1-800-289-0963

The publisher has endeavoured to contact all contributors for permission to reproduce.

A catalogue record for this book is available from the British Library.

ISBN 0 7153 1197 2 hardback
ISBN 0 7153 1906 X paperback

Designed and produced by Penny & Penny
Printed in Singapore by KHL Printing Co Pte Ltd
for David & Charles
Brunel House   Newton Abbot   Devon

Visit our website at www.davidandcharles.co.uk

David & Charles books are available from all good bookshops; alternatively you can contact
our Orderline on (0)1626 334555 or write to us at FREEPOST EX2110, David & Charles Direct,
Newton Abbot, TQ12 4ZZ (no stamp required UK mainland).

Contents

Introduction

If you count up how many cards you send each year you will be amazed at the total: family birthdays; to welcome a new baby; to say have a happy wedding day. Cards when friends are moving house; to wish them good luck in a new job; when they have passed their driving test or have not been well; and for Christmas, cards both traditional and modern. In this book you will find six themed chapters packed with cards for all those occasions and many more beside, and a selection of alphabets to personalize the cards with a name or date. So turn the pages and start celebrating life's special occasions with this unique collection of 136 cards and tags.

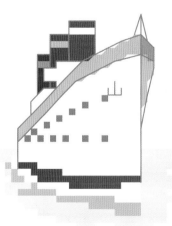

A selection of cards from following chapters clockwise from top left: First birthday teddy, page 20; New job, page 92; Snowy garden, page 78; Spaceship, page 24; Christmas wreath, page 77; Congratulations, page 90; Get well soon, page 94. The tags and place settings can be found on pages 21, 41, 51, 65, 83 and 97.

Welcome Baby

If you know someone who is expecting, then welcome the new baby into the world with a hand-stitched card. Over the next few pages you will find lots of cute cards for baby boys and girls, fun cards for twins and triplets, a Christening card and cards for baby's first birthday, both modern and traditional. Some of the designs have space for stitching baby's name and date of birth, using one of the alphabets on page 98. As well as the cards there are six smaller designs that can be made into gift tags and place settings for a birthday or Christening party. So whether you are stitching for a girl, a boy, twins or even triplets you are sure to find a card to please.

Welcome Baby collection clockwise from top left –
Bonnet & bootees, page 13; Christening sampler, page
18; Stork, page 12; Sleepy bear, page 19; Triplets, page 15;
It's a girl!, page 11. Tags and place settings can be found
on page 21.

Baby boy – Clown

This jolly clown is a great way to welcome a new baby boy in to the family

❖ White Aida, 14 count, 15 x 10.2cm (6 x 4in)
❖ DMC stranded cotton (floss) as listed in the key
❖ Tapestry needle, No 24
❖ Green card with a 11.5 x 7cm (4½ x 2¾in) rectangular opening
❖ Red stick-on sequins
❖ Gold metallic pen

DESIGN SIZE: 7 x 5.2cm (2¾ x 2⅛in).
NOTE: use the gold metallic pen to draw a line around the opening cut in the card. Peel the backing paper off the sequins and attach them to the front of the card just outside the gold line. Full finishing instructions can be found on page 102.

Clown designed by Sam Hawkins

Clown
DMC stranded cotton (floss)

	Xst	BS	FK
Blanc	·		
208	⊠		
310	■	∕	
335	⊟		
349	∪	∕	
722	+		
726	=		
798	↑		
910	⊠		
913	▽		
948	S		
3326	→		

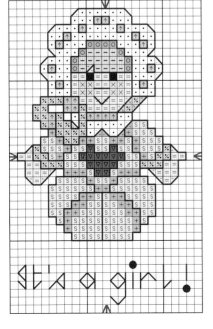

Baby girl – Sugar & spice

As the saying goes 'sugar and spice and all things nice' – two special cards to welcome a new little girl in to the world

❖ White Aida, 14 count 11.5 x 9cm (4½ x 3½in)
❖ DMC stranded cotton (floss) as listed in the key
❖ Tapestry needle, No 24
❖ Lilac card with a 7 x 5.2cm (2¾ x 2⅛in) rectangular opening

DESIGN SIZE: 7 x 5.2cm (2¾ x 2⅛in)
NOTE: the lettering and the pink ribbon ends are backstitched using two strands of stranded cotton (floss).

Sugar and spice designed by Sam Hawkins

Sugar & spice
DMC stranded cotton (floss)

	Xst	BS	FK
209	☒		▨
211	⊟		
335	◪	◩	
543	⊙		
727	+		
776	U		
839	▨	◩	
986	▦	◩	
989	S	◩	
3854	▨		
3864	▽		

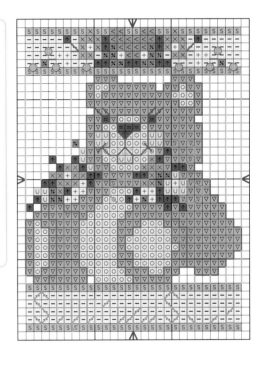

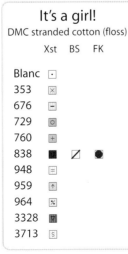

It's a girl!
DMC stranded cotton (floss)

	Xst	BS	FK
Blanc	·		
353	☒		
676	⊟		
729	⊙		
760	+		
838	■	◩	●
948	=		
959	↑		
964	▨		
3328	▼		
3713	S		

It's a girl!

❖ Cream Aida, 14 count 11 x 8.75cm (4⅜ x 3½in)
❖ DMC stranded cotton (floss) as listed in the key
❖ Tapestry needle, No 24
❖ Pink card with a 7 x 5cm (2¾ x 2in) rectangular opening

DESIGN SIZE: 6.8 x 4.3cm (2⅝ x 1⅝in)
NOTE: a matching tag can be found on page 21. It's a girl! is shown stitched on page 8.

It's a girl! designed by Sue Cook

Baby boy – Rocking cradle

After the stork has arrived the new baby will be rocked to sleep by this pretty cradle – two cards to mark the delivery of a special bundle

❖ White evenweave, 28 count 9 x 11cm (3½ x 4½in)
❖ DMC stranded cotton (floss) as listed in the key
❖ DMC metallic thread, antique gold colour 273
❖ Tapestry needle, No 26
❖ Blue card with a 5.6 x 8cm (2¼ x 3⅛in) rectangular opening

DESIGN SIZE: 5 x 7cm (2 x 2¾in)
NOTE: each stitch on the chart is worked over two threads of evenweave. Use a single strand of metallic thread for the backstitch.

Rocking cradle designed by Lesley Teare

Rocking cradle
DMC stranded cotton (floss)

	Xst	BS	FK
819	–		
828	☒		
Gold*		▨	

* DMC antique gold 273

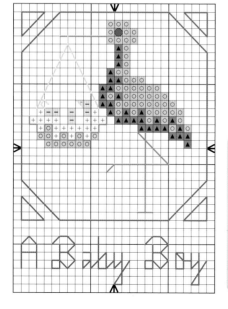

Stork
DMC stranded cotton (floss)

	Xst	BS	FK
3756	+		
3779	–	▨	
3838		▨	●
3839	▲	▨	
3840	◉	▨	

Stork

❖ White Aida, 14 count 11.5 x 9cm (4½ x 3½in)
❖ DMC stranded cotton (floss) as listed in the key
❖ Tapestry needle, No 24
❖ Blue card with a 7 x 5cm (2¾ x 2in) rectangular opening

DESIGN SIZE: 6.25 x 4.5cm (2¼ x 1¾in)
NOTE: a matching tag can be found on page 21. The stork is shown stitched on page 9.

Stork designed by Claire Crompton

Baby girl – Bonnet & bootees

*Pretty green gingham has been used to give this
baby card a country feel – use the alphabet on
page 98 to add the baby's name*

❖ White Aida, 14 count 9 x 11.3cm
  (3½ x 4½in)
❖ DMC stranded cotton (floss) as listed in
  the key
❖ Pink seed beads
❖ Tapestry needle, No 24
❖ White card with a 6 x 8cm (2⅜ x 3⅛in)
  rectangular opening

DESIGN SIZE: 6 x 8cm (2⅜ x 3⅛in)
NOTE: use the alphabet on page 98 to work
a name on the card. The backstitch is
worked using two strands of stranded cotton
(floss). Add the pink beads to the design
in the positions marked on the chart with
pink dots. A matching tag can be found on
page 21.

Bonnet & bootees designed by Maria Diaz

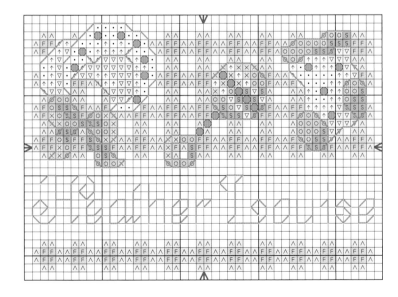

Bonnet and bootees
DMC stranded cotton (floss)

	Xst	BS	FK
Blanc	·		
335		◹	
899	S		
955	∧		
957	O		
963	X		
964	F		
3733			◙ *
3753	▽		
3756	↑		

* DMC seed beads
V1-01-3733 rose pink

Baby birth – Twins

Twice the fun and twice the surprise – this specially designed card is sure to please

❖ Cream Aida, 14 count 20 x 15.5cm (8 x 6¼in)
❖ DMC stranded cotton (floss) as listed in the key
❖ Tapestry needle, No 24
❖ Sky blue card with a 12.5 x 12.5cm (5 x 5in) square opening

DESIGN SIZE: 10.2 x 10.2cm (4 x 4in).
NOTE: this card could also be used for a single birth by adding a name or birth date to the blocks at the bottom of the design. A selection of alphabet and number charts can be found on page 98.

Twins designed by Sue Cook

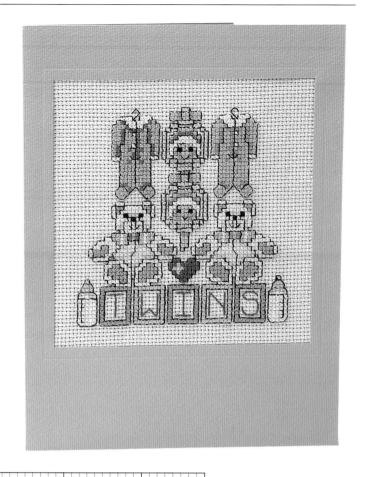

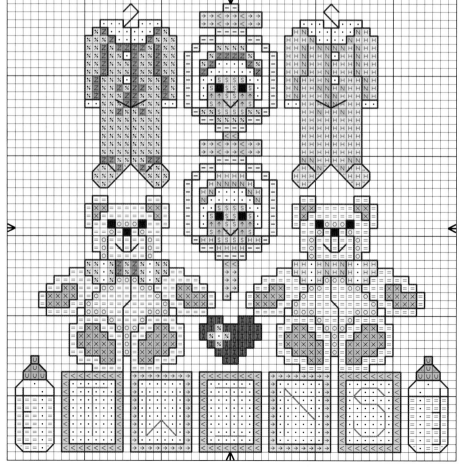

Twins
DMC stranded cotton (floss)

	Xst	BS	FK
Blanc	·		
437	⊠		
727	−		
739	○		
741	U		
746	=		
758	↑		
761	⅓		
838	■	∕	
945	S		
959	◁		
964	→		
3328	⊞	∕	
3712	Z		
3761	H		
3766	N		

Baby birth – Triplets

If you know someone who has given birth to triplets then they are sure to appreciate the unique 3's trouble

❖ White evenweave, 28 count 11 x 15cm
  (4³⁄₈ x 6in)
❖ DMC stranded cotton (floss) as listed
  in the key
❖ Tapestry needle, No 26
❖ Cream card with a 7.2 x 11cm
  (2⁷⁄₈ x 4³⁄₈in) rectangular opening

DESIGN SIZE: 6.5 x 8.7cm (2½ x 3½in)
NOTE: each stitch on the chart is worked over two threads of evenweave fabric. A matching tag can be found on page 21.

Triplets designed by Lesley Teare

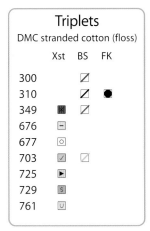

Triplets
DMC stranded cotton (floss)

	Xst	BS	FK
300		◪	
310		◪	●
349	▩	◪	
676	⊟		
677	○		
703	☑	◪	
725	▶		
729	s		
761	U		

Baby birth – Welcome

If you want to start stitching before the baby arrives, soft colours and a traditional design make this card just right for either a boy or girl

❖ Ivory linen, 28 count 15 x 11cm (6 x 4⅜in)
❖ DMC stranded cotton (floss) as listed in the key
❖ Tapestry needle, No 26
❖ Ivory card with a 10.3 x 8cm (4 x 3⅛in) oval opening

DESIGN SIZE: 8.2 x 7cm (3¼ x 2¾in)
NOTE: each stitch on the chart has been worked over two threads of linen.

Welcome designed by Helen Philipps

Welcome			
DMC stranded cotton (floss)			
	Xst	BS	FK
208		◿	
341	⊠		
745	Ⓤ		
3779	⊠		
3813	↑		

Baby birth – Sleepy baby

By changing the ribbon bow from pink to blue, this card can be used for either a boy or girl

❖ Cream Aida, 14 count 16 x 13.5cm (6¼ x 5¼in)
❖ DMC stranded cotton (floss) as listed in the key
❖ Tapestry needle, No 24
❖ Ivory card with a 10 x 10cm (4 x 4in)
    square opening
❖ Pink or blue ribbon bow and wooden heart

DESIGN SIZE: 9 x 7cm (3½ x 2¾in)
NOTE: glue the ribbon bow and wooden heart shape on to the card front centrally below the design. Full finishing instructions can be found on page 102.

Sleepy baby designed by Sue Cook

Sleepy baby
DMC stranded cotton (floss)

	Xst	BS	FK
Blanc	·		
353	⊠		
452	⊟		
453	○		
676	+		
741		╱	
742	U		
744	⊟		
747	↑		
761	⅍		
838			╱
948	▽		
959	S		
964	<		
3712	→		
3766	I		

Christening

This delightful card designed like a traditional sampler will make a wonderful keepsake for baby's special day

❖ Cream linen, 28 count 15 x 11cm (6 x 4⅜in)
❖ DMC stranded cotton (floss) as listed in the key
❖ Tapestry needle, No 26
❖ Silver heart shaped charms x 2
❖ Yellow card with a 11 x 7.2cm (4⅜ x 2⅞in) rectangular opening

DESIGN SIZE: 8.5 x 7cm (3⅜ x 2¾in)
NOTE: each stitch on the chart is worked over two threads of linen. Use the letters from the chart below to add a name to the bottom of the design. The optional heart shaped silver charms are stitched on to the design in the positions marked on the chart with black dots. A matching tag can be found on page 21.

Christening designed by Helen Philipps

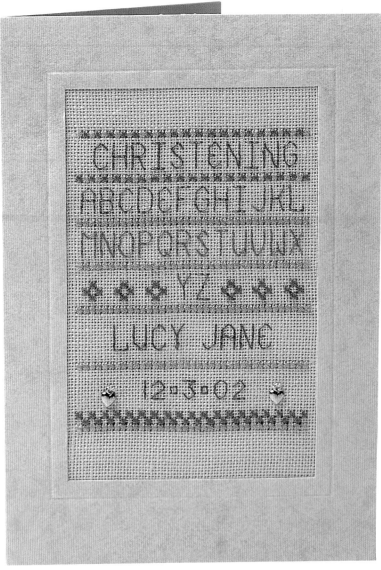

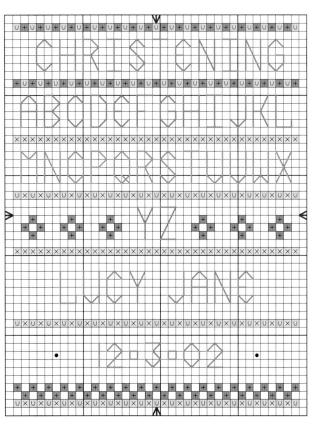

Christening			
DMC stranded cotton (floss)			
	Xst	BS	FK
793		◲	
926		◲	
3778	⊞	◲	
3779	ⓤ		
3813	⊠		

First birthday –
Sleepy bear

This cute bear is a great way to celebrate someone's very first birthday

❖ White Aida, 14 count 14.5 x 13.5cm (5¾ x 5¼in)
❖ DMC stranded cotton (floss) as listed in the key
❖ Tapestry needle, No 24
❖ White card with a 10 x 10cm (4 x 4in) square opening
❖ White daisy trim

DESIGN SIZE: 7 x 8cm (2¾ x 3⅛in)
NOTE: the backstitch is worked in two strands of stranded cotton (floss). Glue the daisy trim to the card front around the opening cut in the card. Full finishing instructions can be found on page 102. A matching tag can be found on page 21.

Sleepy bear designed by Maria Diaz

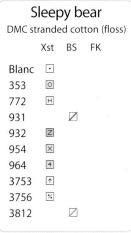

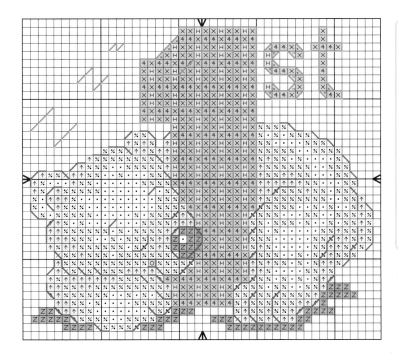

Sleepy bear
DMC stranded cotton (floss)

	Xst	BS	FK
Blanc	·		
353	◎		
772	H		
931		╱	
932	Z		
954	X		
964	4		
3753	↑		
3756	⅍		
3812		╱	

First birthday – Toys

Whether it's a boy who loves toys or a girl who loves teddies, these cards are just right to celebrate a first birthday

❖ White linen, 28 count 15 x 10.4cm (6 x 4⅛in)
❖ DMC stranded cotton (floss) as listed in the key
❖ Tapestry needle, No 26
❖ Bright blue card with a 7.5 x 5.8cm (3 x 2¼in) rectangular opening
❖ Gold metallic pen

DESIGN SIZE: 6.2 x 5.4cm (2½ x 2¼in)
NOTE: each stitch on the chart is worked over two threads of linen. Use the gold metallic pen to draw a line around the opening cut in the card. Full finishing instructions can be found on page 102.

Toys designed by Mari Richards

Toys			
DMC stranded cotton (floss)			
	Xst	BS	FK
Blanc	·		
420	Z	/	
422	–		
666	S	/	
703	N		
726	X		
813	<		
824	H	/	
825	I		
826	→		
945	%		
951	U		
3770	o		
3801	n		◑

Teddy

❖ White evenweave, 28 count 11.5 x 9cm (4½ x 3½in)
❖ DMC stranded cotton (floss) as listed in the key
❖ Tapestry needle, No 26
❖ Beige and pink card with a 8 x 5.5cm (3⅛ x 2¼in) rectangular opening

DESIGN SIZE: 6 x 4cm (2⅜ x 1½in)
NOTE: each stitch on the chart is worked over two threads of evenweave. Turn to page 102 for mounting and finishing instructions. Teddy is shown stitched on page 6.

First birthday teddy designed by Lesley Teare

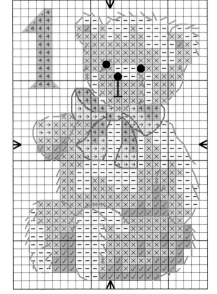

Teddy			
DMC stranded cotton (floss)			
	Xst	BS	FK
310		/	●
676	X		
677	–		
729	/		
760	4		
782		/	
3713	→		
3328		/	

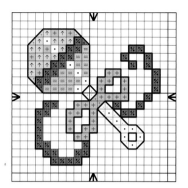

It's a girl!
DMC stranded cotton (floss)

	Xst	BS	FK
Blanc	·		
760	+		
838		╱	
959	=		
964	↑		
3328	▨		

The it's a girl! tag can be seen stitched with its matching card on page 8. The card chart can be found on page 11. Designed by Sue Cook.

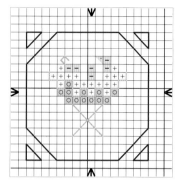

Stork
DMC stranded cotton (floss)

	Xst	BS	FK
3756	⊞		
3779	⊟	╱	
3838		╱	
3839		╱	
3840	○		

The stork tag can be seen stitched with its matching card on page 9. The card chart can be found on page 12. Designed by Claire Crompton.

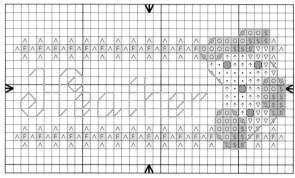

Bonnet and bootees
DMC stranded cotton (floss)

	Xst	BS	FK
Blanc	·		
335		╱	
899	S		
955	∧		
957	○		
964	F		
3753	▽		
3756	↑		
Beads*	▨		

*DMC seed beads:
V1-01-3733

The bonnet and bootees place setting can be seen stitched with its matching card on page 8. The card chart can be found on page 13, and the alphabet for this design on page 98. Designed by Maria Diaz.

Turn to the matching card chart pages for details of the fabric used in making these tags. General finishing instructions can be found on page 102.

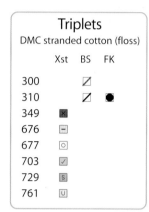

Triplets
DMC stranded cotton (floss)

	Xst	BS	FK
300		╱	
310		╱	●
349	▨		
676	⊟		
677	○		
703	╱		
729	S		
761	U		

The triplets tag can be seen stitched with its matching card on page 8. The card chart can be found on page 15. Designed by Lesley Teare.

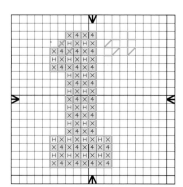

Sleepy bear
DMC stranded cotton (floss)

	Xst	BS	FK
772	H		
954	✕		
964	4		
3812		╱	

The sleepy bear tag can be seen stitched with its matching card on page 9. The card chart can be found on page 19. Designed by Maria Diaz.

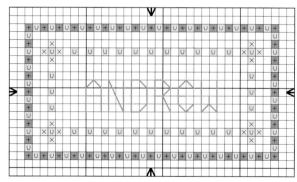

Christening
DMC stranded cotton (floss)

	Xst	BS	FK
793		╱	
3778	⊞		
3779	U		
3813	✕		

The Christening place setting can be seen stitched with its matching card on page 8. The card chart can be found on page 18, and the alphabet on page 98. Designed by Helen Philipps.

Happy Birthday

There can be no nicer way to say happy birthday than with a hand-stitched card. Printed cards can be very costly, and so making your own will not only save money, but give you the pleasure of sending a special gift. In this chapter you will find fun cards for boys; pretty cards for girls; cool cards for teenagers; family cards for mum, dad, sister, brother; cards for people with passions like sailing, gardening, fishing, cooking, and cricket; and cards for landmark birthdays like 60th or 70th. In fact, whatever birthday card you are looking for, be it big, small, square, circular, modern or traditional, you are sure to find it in this great selection of birthday cards and tags.

Happy Birthday collection clockwise from top left – Party frock, page 29; 70th birthday, page 39; Out to play, page 26; Brother's birthday, page 30; Little princess, page 27; Singing bluebird, page 32. Tags and place settings can be found on page 41.

Boy's birthday – Racing car

Budding racing drivers or astronauts will love this Formula One car or spaceship for their birthday

❖ White Aida, 14 count 15 x 11cm (6 x 4⅜in)
❖ DMC stranded cotton (floss) as listed in the key
❖ Tapestry needle, No 24
❖ Sunflower yellow card with a 8.3cm (3¼in) diameter circular opening

DESIGN SIZE: 7 x 5cm (2¾ x 2in)
NOTE: use the chart on page 98 to work the number on the bonnet of the racing car.

Racing car designed by Maria Diaz

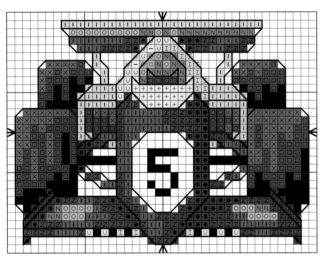

Racing car
DMC stranded cotton (floss)

	Xst	BS	FK		Xst	BS	FK		Xst	BS	FK
307	U			415	I			817	Z		
310	■	╱		444	I			995	N		
350	▮			445	–			996	O		
413	▦			498	●						
414	✕			747	+						

Spaceship

❖ Pale blue Aida, 14 count 11.5 x 9cm (4½ x 3½in)
❖ DMC stranded cotton (floss) as listed in the key
❖ Silver metallic thread
❖ Tapestry needle, No 24
❖ Grey blue and blue card with a 8 x 5.5cm (3¼ x 2¼in) rectangular opening

DESIGN SIZE: 6.3 x 4cm (2½ x 1½in)
NOTE: use the numbers chart on page 98 to work the birthday year at the bottom of the design. Turn to page 102 for mounting and finishing instructions. The spaceship is shown stitched on page 7.

Spaceship designed by Claire Crompton

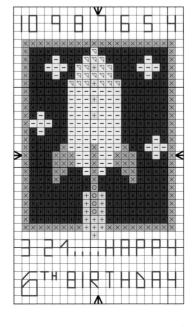

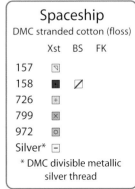

Spaceship
DMC stranded cotton (floss)

	Xst	BS	FK
157	◳		
158	■	╱	
726	+		
799	✕		
972	O		
Silver*	–		

* DMC divisible metallic silver thread

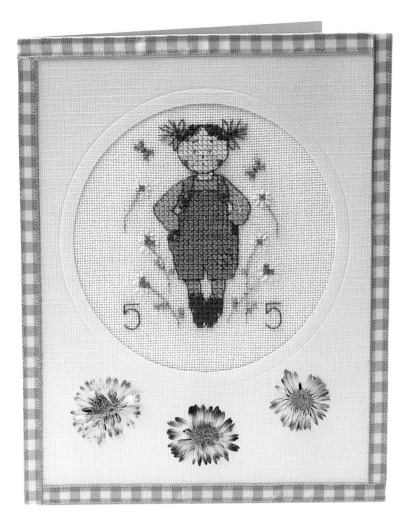

Girl's birthday – Daisy

*Send a special little girl this pretty pink card
with real pressed flowers and a ribbon trim*

❖ Ivory evenweave, 28 count 16.7 x 13.5cm
  (6½ x 5¼in)
❖ DMC stranded cotton (floss) as listed in the key
❖ Tapestry needle, No 26
❖ Pastel pink card with a 9.5cm (3¾in) diameter
  circular opening
❖ Pink gingham ribbon and pressed flowers

DESIGN SIZE: 7.5 x 6cm (3 x 2⅜in)
NOTE: each stitch on the chart is worked over two
threads of evenweave. Use the numbers chart on
page 98 to work the girl's age at the bottom of the
design. Glue the ribbon around the outer edge of
the card and decorate the front with pressed flowers.
Full finishing instructions can be found on page 102

Daisy designed by Lesley Teare

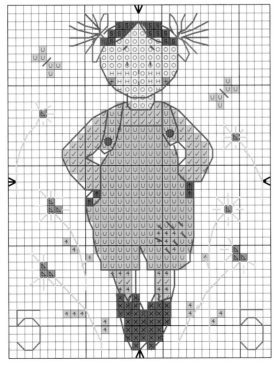

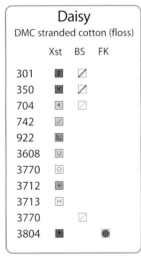

Daisy
DMC stranded cotton (floss)

	Xst	BS	FK
301	▩	◹	
350	▨	◹	
704	4	◹	
742	◹		
922	◰		
3608	U		
3770	○		
3712	⊞		
3713	H		
3770		◹	
3804	▩		◉

Boy's birthday – Out to play

Here's a card that is sure to suit the boy who loves to play outdoors

❖ White evenweave, 28 count 15 x 11cm (6 x 4¼in)
❖ DMC stranded cotton (floss) as listed in the key
❖ Tapestry needle, No 26
❖ Blue card with a 10 x 8cm (4 x 3⅛in) oval opening

DESIGN SIZE: 7.6 x 5.6cm (3 x 2¼in)
NOTE: each stitch on the chart is worked over two threads of evenweave. Use the alphabet on page 98 to stitch a name on the design. A matching tag can be found on page 41.

Out to play designed by Lesley Teare

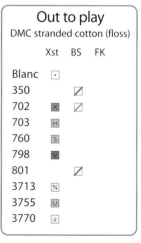

Out to play

DMC stranded cotton (floss)

	Xst	BS	FK
Blanc	·		
350		⊘	
702	⊠	⊘	
703	H		
760	S		
798	▼		
801		⊘	
3713	⁒		
3755	U		
3770	↓		

Girl's birthday – Teddy's party

Your own little princess is sure to love either of these pretty cards

❖ White linen, 30 count 11.5 x 9cm (4½ x 3½in)
❖ DMC stranded cotton (floss) as listed in the key
❖ Tapestry needle, No 26
❖ Lilac card with a 7cm (2¾in) diameter circular opening

DESIGN SIZE: 5.5 x 5cm (2¼ x 2in)
NOTE: each stitch on the chart is worked over two threads of white linen. Use the numbers chart on page 98 to work the birthday year on the design.

Teddy's party designed by Susan Penny

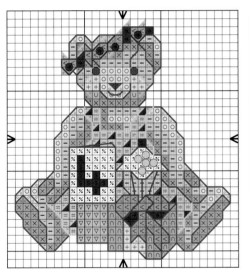

Teddy's party
DMC stranded cotton (floss)

	Xst	BS	FK		Xst	BS	FK
436	☒			760	U		
554	▤	╱		761	+		
600	■	╱		844	▨		●
601	■			898		╱	
603	◰			3348	▽	╱	
738	▭		▥	3839	⋒		
739	◯			3865	⦂		

Little princess

❖ White Aida, 14 count 11.5 x 9cm (4½ x 3½in)
❖ DMC stranded cotton (floss) as listed in the key
❖ Tapestry needle, No 24
❖ Blue card with a 8 x 5.6cm (3⅛ x 2¼in) rectangular opening

DESIGN SIZE: 6.7 x 5cm (2⅝ x 2in)
NOTE: use the alphabet on page 98 to stitch a name on the design. Little princess is shown stitched on page 22. A matching tag can be found on page 41 .

Little princess designed by Claire Crompton

Little princess
DMC stranded cotton (floss)

	Xst	BS	FK
Blanc	·		☐
151	N		▥
153	◯		
157	↓		
164	◩		
209	▨	╱	
722	◪		◉
744	U		
948	C		
3804	▦	╱	●
3839	▨		

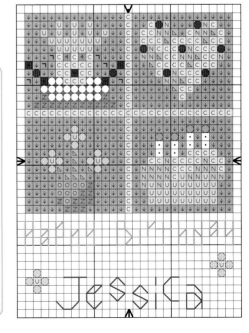

Teenage boy – Cool day

Finding the right card for a teenager can be difficult, so here's one for a cool kid

❖ Ecru Aida, 14 count 15 x 10.5cm (6 x 4⅛in)
❖ DMC stranded cotton (floss) as listed in the key
❖ Tapestry needle, No 24
❖ Navy card with a 11.4 x 7cm (4½ x 2¾in) rectangular opening
❖ Gold metallic pen

DESIGN SIZE: 9 x 6.2cm (3½ x 2½in)
NOTE: use the gold metallic pen to draw a line around the opening cut in the card. Finishing and mounting instructions can be found on page 102.

Cool day designed by Sue Cook

Cool day
DMC stranded cotton (floss)

	Xst	BS	FK
Blanc	·		
318	⊠		
415	Ū		
503	═		
712	↑		
738	⅍		
741	▽		
743	S		
758	<		
824	◆		
826	I		
827	Z		
838	■	╱	
970	N		
3799	✦		

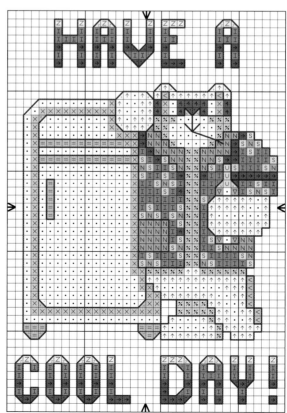

Teenage girl – Pretty in pink

Teenagers love to dress up for a girls' night out: these cards are a celebration of party finery

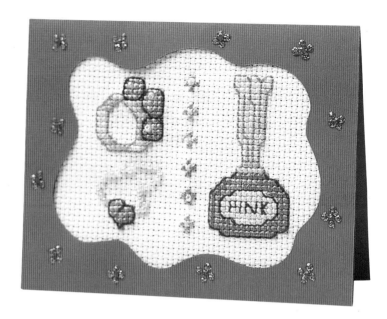

❖ White Aida, 14 count 9 x 11.5cm (3½ x 4½in)
❖ DMC stranded cotton (floss) as listed in the key
❖ Pale tangerine seed beads
❖ Tapestry needle, No 24
❖ Pink card with a 7 x 9.2cm (2¾ x 3⅝in) shaped opening
❖ Gold and pink glitter glue

DESIGN SIZE: 5.2 x 7cm (2⅛ x 2¾in)
NOTE: all the backstitch is done using two strands of stranded cotton (floss). Add the pale tangerine beads to the stitching in the positions marked on the chart with a yellow dot. Use the trace on page 109, and the finishing instructions on page 102 to cut the shaped card mount. Apply dots of glitter glue in patterns on to the front of the card.

Pretty in pink designed by Maria Diaz

Pretty in pink and party frock
DMC stranded cotton (floss)

	Xst	BS	FK		Xst	BS	FK
209	4			742	F		
552		◪		744	S		▥ *
554	H			745	÷		
600		◪		958	←		
603	U			959			▥ **
604	O			964	✕		
740		◪		3808		◪	

DMC seed beads: * V1-06-744 pale tangerine
** V1-04-959 aqua

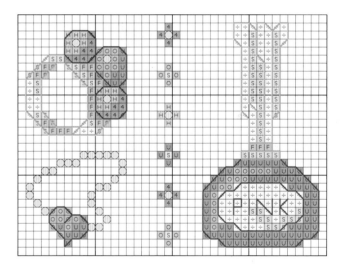

Party frock

❖ White Aida, 14 count 9 x 11.5cm (3½ x 4½in)
❖ DMC stranded cotton (floss) as listed in the key
❖ Aqua seed beads
❖ Tapestry needle, No 24
❖ Mauve card with a 7 x 9cm (2¾ x 3½in) shaped opening
❖ Pink and green glitter glue

DESIGN SIZE: 5.2 x 6.8cm (2⅛ x 2⅝in)
NOTE: all the backstitch is done using two strands of stranded cotton (floss). Add the aqua beads to the stitching in the positions marked on the chart with an aqua dot. Use the trace on page 109 to cut the shaped card mount. Add a line of pink and green glitter glue around the shaped opening in the front of the card. A matching tag can be found on page 41. Party frock is shown stitched on page 22.

Party frock designed by Maria Diaz

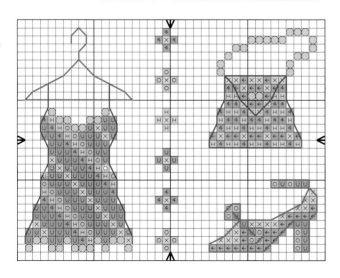

Dad's birthday – Sailing away

Even if dad has never been sailing, he is sure to love this card decorated with a blue anchor

❖ White evenweave, 28 count 10 x 15cm (4 x 6in)
❖ DMC stranded cotton (floss) as listed in the key
❖ Tapestry needle, No 26
❖ White card with a 5.5 x 7.5cm (2¼ x 3in) rectangular opening
❖ Gold metallic pen, blue felt-tipped pen

DESIGN SIZE: 6 x 7cm (2⅜ x 2¾in)
NOTE: each stitch on the chart is worked over two threads of evenweave. Use the gold metallic pen to draw a line around the opening on the front of the card. Use the trace on page 109 and the blue felt-tipped pen to draw an anchor on the card. More detailed instructions for decorating cards can be found on page 102.

Sailing away designed by Mari Richards

Sailing away
DMC stranded cotton (floss)

	Xst	BS	FK		Xst	BS	FK
Blanc	·			799	◎		
420	▦			800	⊠		
422	→			809	⊟		
797	▲	⁄		809*	◄		
798	▦			869	▨	⁄	

* Half cross stitch

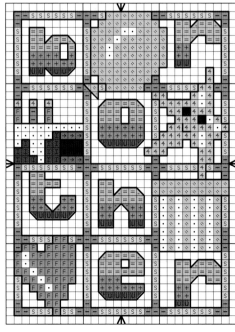

Party fun
DMC stranded cotton (floss)

	Xst	BS	FK
Blanc	·		
166	▧		
433	▣		
435	→		
608	▥		
725	◢		
740	+		
742	⊟		
838	■	⁄	
3833	▣		
3844	▤		
3846	⑤		

Brother's birthday –
Party fun

Whatever his age, your brother will love this jolly card with cake, balloon and happy star

❖ White Aida, 14 count 11.5 x 9cm (4½ x 3½in)
❖ DMC stranded cotton (floss) as listed in the key
❖ Tapestry needle, No 24
❖ Yellow card with a 7 x 5cm (2¾ x 2in) rectangular opening

DESIGN SIZE: 7 x 5cm (2¾ x 2in)
NOTE: this card is shown stitched on page 23. A matching tag can be found on page 41.

Party fun designed by Sue Cook

Man's birthday –
Gone fishing

If you are a fisherman's friend, here's the perfect greeting to wish him a great day

❖ White Aida, 14 count 15 x 11cm (6 x 4⅜in)
❖ DMC stranded cotton (floss) as listed in the key
❖ Tapestry needle, No 24
❖ Green card with a 10 x 8cm (4 x 3⅛in) oval opening

DESIGN SIZE: 9 x 7.5cm (3½ x 3in)
NOTE: backstitch the lettering in two strands of stranded cotton (floss).

Gone fishing designed by Maria Diaz

Gone fishing
DMC stranded cotton (floss)

	Xst	BS	FK
435	+		
436	N		
498		◪	
676	⊠		
677	−		
800	+		
898	■	◪	
927	△		
3346	◢		
3347	Z		
3774	F		
3820	S		
3822	○		

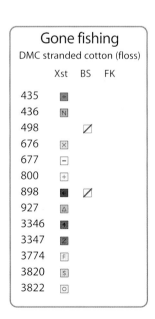

Sister's birthday – Flower vase

If you can't send flowers, then this vase of pink and yellow blooms is the next best thing

❖ Cream linen, 28 count 15 x 11cm (6 x 4⅜in)
❖ DMC stranded cotton (floss) as listed in the key
❖ Tapestry needle, No 26
❖ Pale lavender card with a 8cm (3⅛in) diameter circular opening

DESIGN SIZE: 6.7 x 4.5cm (2⅝ x 1¾in)
NOTE: each stitch on the chart is worked over two threads of linen.

Flower vase designed by Mari Richards

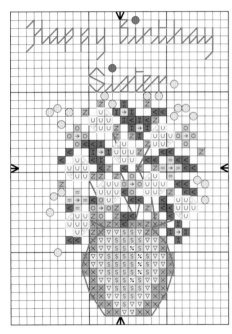

Flower vase
DMC stranded cotton (floss)

	Xst	BS	FK
208		◻	
209	⊠		
210	⊡		
211	▽		
444	→	◻	▥
445	∪		
987	◪	◻	
989	Ɀ		
3607	I	◻	◉
3608	⊙		
3609	▤		
3865	▨		

Mum's birthday – Singing bluebird

Sing the praises of a very special mum by sending her this pretty bluebird card

❖ White evenweave, 28 count 11.5 x 9cm (4½ x 3½in)
❖ DMC stranded cotton (floss) as listed in the key
❖ Tapestry needle, No 26
❖ Cream card with a 8 x 5.5cm (3⅛ x 2¼in) rectangular opening

DESIGN SIZE: 6.5 x 4.5cm (2½ x 1¾in)
NOTE: each stitch on the chart is worked over two threads of evenweave. This card is shown stitched on page 22. A matching tag can be found on page 41.

Singing bluebird designed by Lesley Teare

Singing bluebird
DMC stranded cotton (floss)

	Xst	BS	FK		Xst	BS	FK
Blanc	·			977	+		
155	⊠			3814	∪	◻	
310	■	◻	●	3820	▤		
734	▤	◻		3822	↑		
746	◻			3838	▨		
791	▼						

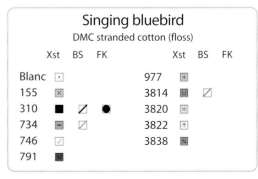

General birthday – Garden cottage

This charming scene makes an ideal card for anyone with a real passion for gardening

❖ Light green linen, 28 count 20 x 15.5cm (8 x 6¼in)
❖ DMC stranded cotton (floss) as listed in the key
❖ Tapestry needle, No 26
❖ Lavender card with a 12.5cm (5in) diameter circular opening

DESIGN SIZE: 9.5 x 9.5cm (3¾ x 3¾in).
NOTE: each stitch on the chart is worked over two threads of linen. The french knots used for the wisteria could be replaced with lavender coloured seed beads.

Garden cottage designed by Susan Penny

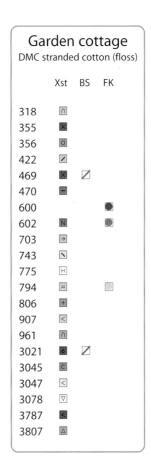

Garden cottage
DMC stranded cotton (floss)

	Xst	BS	FK
318	⌂		
355	✕		
356	⊘		
422	⊘		
469	✕	⁄	
470	⊟		
600			●
602	N		◐
703	→		
743	◩		
775	H		
794	≡		▨
806	+		
907	◁		
961	⋒		
3021	✶	⁄	
3045	⊂		
3047	◁		
3078	▽		
3787	✕		
3807	△		

General birthday – Cricket

Knock a cricket mad friend for six with this
delightful celebration of that unique game

❖ Pastel green Aida, 14 count 15 x 11cm (6 x 4⅜in)
❖ DMC stranded cotton (floss) as listed in the key
❖ Tapestry needle, No 24
❖ Beige card with a 11 x 7cm (4⅜ x 2¾in)
   rectangular opening

DESIGN SIZE: 8.5 x 6.5cm (3⅜ x 2½in)
NOTE: turn to the alphabets on page 98 if you would
like to add a team name to the bottom of the design.

Cricket designed by Maria Diaz

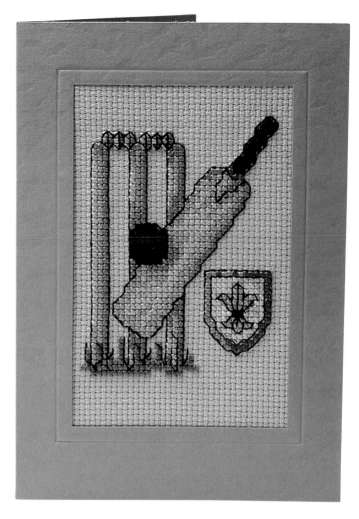

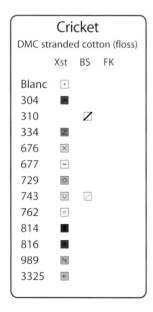

Cricket

DMC stranded cotton (floss)

	Xst	BS	FK
Blanc	⋅		
304	▦		
310		◪	
334	▨		
676	⊠		
677	−		
729	○		
743	U	◩	
762	═		
814	■		
816	▦		
989	N		
3325	←		

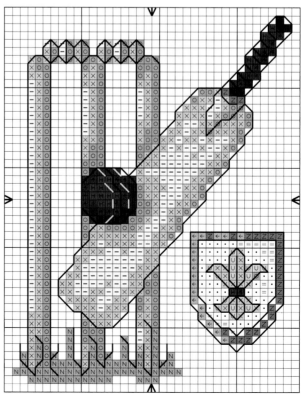

General birthday –
Sewing

If you know a keen stitcher, here's a great way to show you share their passion

❖ White Aida, 14 count 11 x 15cm (4⅜ x 6in)
❖ DMC stranded cotton (floss) as listed in the key
❖ Tapestry needle, No 24
❖ Sage green card with a 7 x 11cm (2¾ x 4⅜in) rectangular opening

DESIGN SIZE: 7 x 9.5cm (2¾ x 3¾in)
NOTE: use two strands of stranded cotton (floss) to backstitch the wool ends hanging from the basket at the bottom of the design.

Sewing designed by Claire Crompton

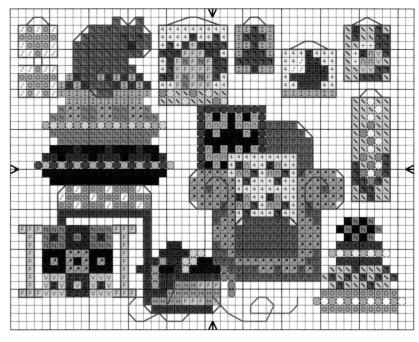

Sewing
DMC stranded cotton (floss)

	Xst	BS	FK
151	V		
154	✖		●
155	N		●
434	◪		
436	H		
738	F		
797	◄		
799	I		
800	4		□
819	+		
898	▨	╱	
904	◪		
3041	▽		
3042	↗		
3348	◺		
3733	∩		
3803	▨	╱	●
3823	╱		□
3826	◪		
3834	■	╱	
3852	◙		

General birthday – Cooking

Some people just like to eat, while others like to spend every spare minute creating something yummy. Here's a card for the passionate cook

❖ White Aida, 14 count 15 x 11cm (6 x 4 3/8in)
❖ DMC stranded cotton (floss) as listed in the key
❖ Tapestry needle, No 24
❖ Pink card with a 10.5 x 8cm (4⅛ x 3⅛in) oval opening

DESIGN SIZE: 7.5 x 6cm (3 x 2⅜in)
NOTE: the french knots used to decorate the pudding dishes could be replaced with seed beads.

Cooking designed by Claire Crompton

Cooking

DMC stranded cotton (floss)

	Xst	BS	FK		Xst	BS	FK
Blanc	·			963	+		□
164	F			988	◣		
334	N			3325	U	◩	
340	⊠		▨	3733	I		▨
725	<			3746	Z		
758	C			3778	H		
780	▼			3803	M		▨
782	○			3830	⊓		
798	T		▨	3855	⊟		
938		◪					

General birthday – Sailing

Capture the spirit of the sea as a reminder of happy days afloat, for a friend whose favourite days are spent under sail

❖ Light blue linen, 28 count 15 x 11cm (6 x 4⅜in)
❖ DMC stranded cotton (floss) as listed in the key
❖ Tapestry needle, No 26
❖ White card with a 10.5 x 8cm (4⅛ x 3⅛in) oval opening

DESIGN SIZE: 7.8 x 6.5cm (3 x 2⅝in)
NOTE: each stitch on the chart is worked over two threads of linen.

Sailing designed by Sam Hawkins

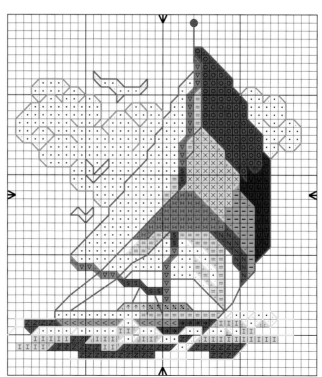

Sailing			
DMC stranded cotton (floss)			
	Xst	BS	FK
Blanc	·		
221	▣		
223	<		
312	N		
321	O		
334	H	◪	
413		◪	
415	=		
435	▽		
561	Z		
563	I	◪	
676	↑		
726	⊠		
729	⅔		
783	–		
801	S	◪	◉
814	▪		

40th birthday

*Bring a smile to the face of anyone who has
reached this landmark in life*

❖ Cream Aida, 14 count 11.5 x 15cm (4½ x 6in)
❖ DMC stranded cotton (floss) as listed in the key
❖ Tapestry needle, No 24
❖ Aqua card with a 8.5 x 10.5cm (3⅜ x 4⅛in) shaped
  opening
❖ Multi-coloured shiny paper

DESIGN SIZE: 6.3 x 8cm (2½ x 3⅛in)
NOTE: use the trace on page 109, and the finishing
instructions on page 102 to cut the shaped card mount.
Decorate the mount with small squares of shiny paper.

40th birthday designed by Sue Cook

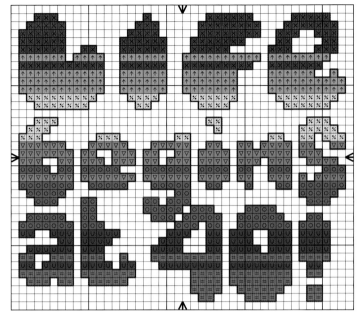

40th birthday
DMC stranded cotton (floss)

	Xst	BS	FK
321	▨		
322	◉		
336	▨		
553	▥		
740	↑		
743	⁒		
838		╱	
911	▽		

60th birthday

A 60th birthday can be a big milestone – this pretty card is a reminder of the happy days gone and the many more that are yet to come

- White linen, 28 count 15 x 10.5cm (6 x 4⅛in)
- DMC stranded cotton (floss) as listed in the key
- Tapestry needle, No 26
- White card with a 7.5 x 5.7cm (3 x 2¼in) rectangular opening
- Bronze metallic felt-tipped pen

DESIGN SIZE: 6.5 x 5cm (2½ x 2in)
NOTE: each stitch on the chart is worked over two threads of linen. Use the bronze metallic pen to draw a line around the opening cut in the card.

60th birthday designed by Mari Richards

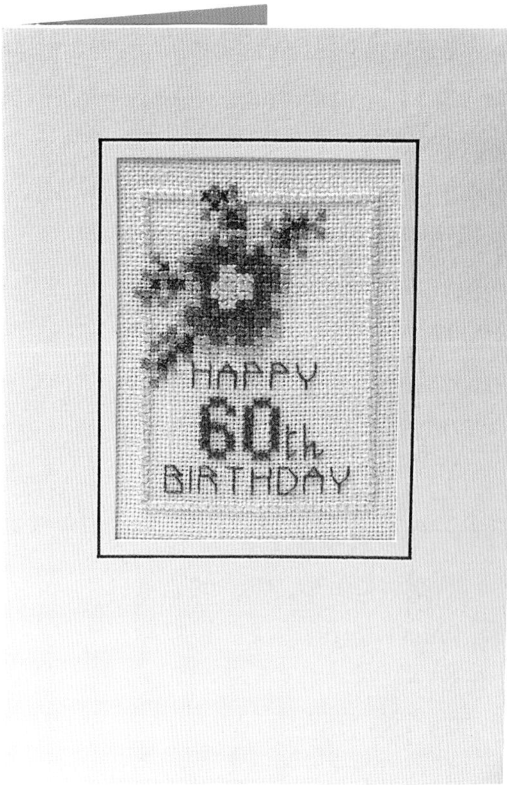

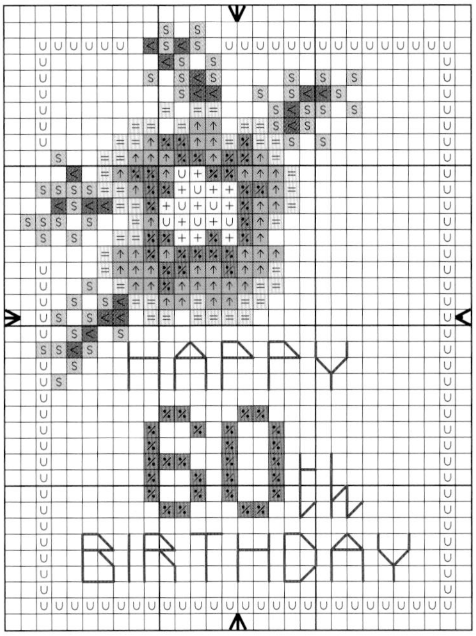

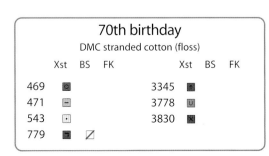

60th birthday
DMC stranded cotton (floss)

	Xst	BS	FK
Ecru	+		
367	<		
368	S		
760	↑		
3712	✕	⁄	
3713	=		
3823	U		

70th birthday

Now is the time of the third age. Celebrate three score years and ten with this unique card

- Cream Aida, 14 count 9 x 11.5cm (3⅝ x 4½in)
- DMC stranded cotton (floss) as listed in the key
- Tapestry needle, No 24
- Beige card with a 5.5 x 8cm (2¼ x 3⅛in) rectangular opening

DESIGN SIZE: 4.5 x 6.7cm (1¾ x 2⅝in)
NOTE: this card is shown stitched on page 22. A matching tag can be found on page 41.

70th birthday designed by Claire Crompton

70th birthday
DMC stranded cotton (floss)

	Xst	BS	FK		Xst	BS	FK
469	O			3345	↑		
471	−			3778	U		
543	·			3830	✕		
779	⌐	⁄					

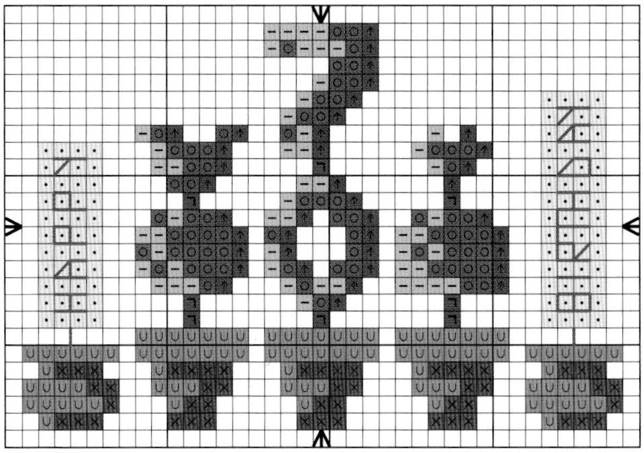

General birthday – Postage stamp

This unusual card can be adapted to celebrate any birthday by adding the year to the design

❖ White Aida, 14 count 15 x 10.5cm (6 x 4⅛in)
❖ DMC stranded cotton (floss) as listed in the key
❖ Tapestry needle, No 24
❖ Cream card with a 10 x 8cm (4 x 3⅛in)
   rectangular opening

DESIGN SIZE: 9.3 x 7.2cm (3⅝ x 2⅞in)
NOTE: use the numbers chart on page 98 to add the age
of the recipient.

Postage stamp designed by Susan Penny

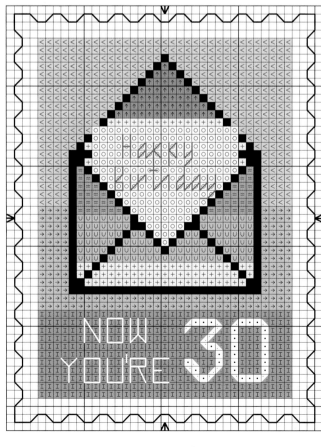

Postage stamp			
DMC stranded cotton (floss)			
	Xst	BS	FK
Blanc	·	◪	
Ecru	○		
310	■	◪	
666		◪	
747	+		
806	↑		
807	=		
958	I		
959	→		
964	<		
3766	U		

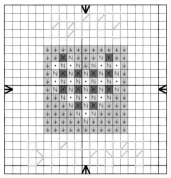

Out to play
DMC stranded cotton (floss)

	Xst	BS	FK
Blanc	·		
350	◿		
702	◿		
798	⊠		

The out to play place setting can be seen stitched with its matching card on page 23. The card chart can be found on page 26, and the alphabet on page 98. Designed by Lesley Teare.

Little princess
DMC stranded cotton (floss)

	Xst	BS	FK
Blanc	·		
151	N		
157	↓		
209		◿	
3804	⊠		

The little princess tag can be seen stitched with its matching card on page 22. The card chart can be found on page 27, and the alphabet on page 98. Designed by Claire Crompton.

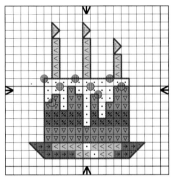

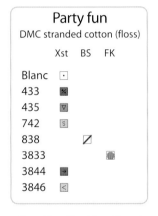

Party fun
DMC stranded cotton (floss)

	Xst	BS	FK
Blanc	·		
433	⊠		
435	▽		
742	S		
838		◿	
3833			▦
3844	➡		
3846	◁		

The party fun tag can be seen stitched with its matching card on page 23. The card chart can be found on page 30. Designed by Sue Cook.

Turn to the matching card chart pages for details of the fabric used in making these tags. General finishing instructions can be found on page 102.

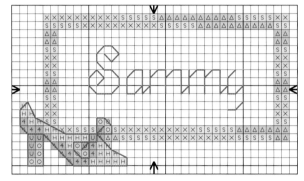

The party frock place setting can be seen stitched with its matching card on page 22. The card chart can be found on page 29, and the alphabet on page 98. Designed by Maria Diaz.

Party frock
DMC stranded cotton (floss)

	Xst	BS	FK
209	⊞		
552		◿	
554	H		
603	U		
604	O		
954	S		
964	⊠		
3766	△		

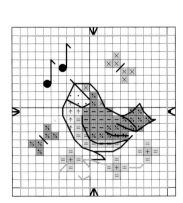

Singing bluebird
DMC stranded cotton (floss)

	Xst	BS	FK
Blanc	·		
155	⊠		
310		◿	●
734	➡	◿	
977	⊞		
3820	⊟		
3822	⬆		
3838	⊠		

The singing bluebird tag can be seen stitched with its matching card on page 22. The card chart can be found on page 32. Designed by Lesley Teare.

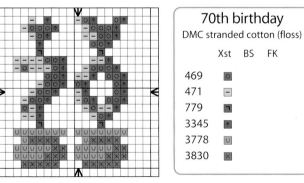

70th birthday
DMC stranded cotton (floss)

	Xst	BS	FK
469	◙		
471	−		
779	⬎		
3345	⊠		
3778	U		
3830	⊠		

The 70th birthday tag can be seen stitched with its matching card on page 22. The card chart can be found on page 39. Designed by Claire Crompton.

Weddings and Anniversaries

Weddings and anniversaries are occasions when a hand-stitched card will be treasured forever. The happy couple – whether newly married or married for many years – will appreciate the effort you have put into the stitching. In this chapter you will also find designs for people getting engaged, or those who celebrate Valentine's Day, as well as a selection of cards for silver, gold, ruby and diamond anniversaries. For the newly married there are wedding flowers, a cake and a beautiful bride with a beaded dress, as well as a selection of designs for gift tags and place settings – a complete collection for the happy couple.

Weddings and Anniversaries collection clockwise from top left – Silver wedding, page 49; Bride, page 47; Swans, page 45; Valentine's day, page 44; Health & happiness, page 46; Diamond wedding, page 50. Tags and place settings can be found on page 51.

Valentine's day

Send this pretty Valentine's card with love, to that extra special person in your life

❖ Pastel Pink linen, 28 count 15 x 11cm (6 x4¼in)
❖ DMC stranded cotton (floss) as listed in the key
❖ Tapestry needle, No 26
❖ Pale pink card with a 11 x 7.2cm (4⅜ x 2⅞in) rectangular opening

DESIGN SIZE: 8.2 x 6.4cm (3¼ x 2½in)
NOTE: each stitch on the chart is worked over two threads of linen. A matching tag can be found on page 51.

Valentine's day designed by Helen Philipps

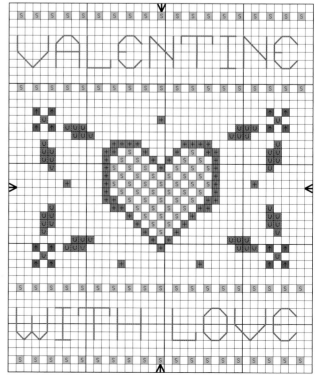

Valentine's day
DMC stranded cotton (floss)

	Xst	BS	FK
315		⤢	
793	↑		
962	S		
3052	ᵾ		
3607	+		

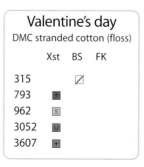

Engagement – Diamond ring

Either of these cards will make a wonderful keepsake, add initials or a date using one of the alphabets on page 98

❖ Cream Aida, 14 count 15 x 10.5cm (6 x 4⅛in)
❖ DMC stranded cotton (floss) as listed in the key
❖ Tapestry needle, No 24
❖ Cream card with a 7.5 x 5.7cm (3 x 2¼in) rectangular opening
❖ Gold metallic pen

DESIGN SIZE: 6.6 x 4.8cm (2⅝ x 1⅞in)
NOTE: use the gold metallic pen to draw a line around the opening cut in the card.

Diamond ring designed by Sue Cook

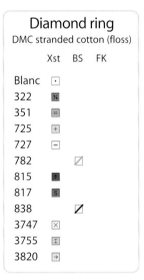

Diamond ring
DMC stranded cotton (floss)

	Xst	BS	FK
Blanc	·		
322	▨		
351	▤		
725	+		
727	−		
782		◿	
815	◪		
817	S		
838		◿	
3747	☒		
3755	I		
3820	◈		

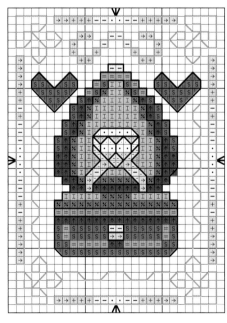

Swans

❖ Pale blue evenweave, 28 count 12.5 x 12.5cm (5 x 5in)
❖ DMC stranded cotton (floss) as listed in the key
❖ DMC metallic thread, antique gold colour 273
❖ Tapestry needle, No 26
❖ White card with a 7.5 x 7.5cm (3 x 3in) square opening
❖ Clear flat-backed jewel shapes

DESIGN SIZE: 4.6 x 6.5cm (1¾ x 2½in)
NOTE: each stitch on the chart is worked over two threads of evenweave. Glue a jewel to the front of the card, above and below the stitching. Swans can be seen stitched on page 43. A matching tag can be found on page 51.

Swans designed by Lesley Teare

Swans
DMC stranded cotton (floss)

	Xst	BS	FK
B5200	☒		
Gold*		◿	

* DMC antique gold 273

Wedding – Floral wreath

Send your best wishes for a happy day and future life together with one of these pretty stitched cards

❖ Antique white linen, 28 count 11.5 x 9cm (4½ x 3⅝in)
❖ DMC stranded cotton (floss) as listed in the key
❖ Tapestry needle, No 26
❖ Peach card with a 7cm (2¾in) diameter circular opening

DESIGN SIZE: 5.5 x 5.5cm (2¼ x 2¼in).
NOTE: each stitch on the chart is stitched over two threads of linen.

Floral wreath designed by Anne Wilson

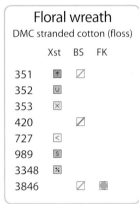

Floral wreath
DMC stranded cotton (floss)

	Xst	BS	FK
351	↑	◸	
352	U		
353	✕		
420		◸	
727	<		
989	S		
3348	✕		
3846		◸	◻

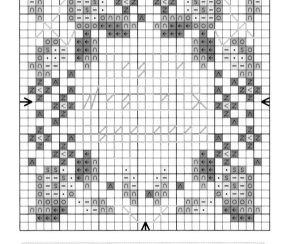

Health & happiness

❖ White Aida, 11 count 15 x 11cm (6 x 4⅜in)
❖ DMC stranded cotton (floss) as listed in the key
❖ Seed beads in the colours listed in the key
❖ Tapestry needle, No 24
❖ White card with a 7.5 x 7.5cm (3 x 3in) square opening

DESIGN SIZE: 12 x 7.5cm (4¾ x 3in).
NOTE: use two strands of stranded cotton for the backstitch and for attaching the beads. Health & happiness is shown stitched on page 42. A matching tag can be found on page 51.

Health & happiness designed by Claire Crompton

Health & happiness
DMC stranded cotton (floss)

	Xst	BS	FK		Xst	BS	FK
316✦	S			832		◸	
702★	←			963★	⊟		
704★	⋂	◸		3047✦	<		
793✦	Z			3733*	⊡		
818*	·			3746*	⋀		

DMC beads:
* V1 seed beads ✦ V2 Nostalgia beads
★ V4 Frosted beads

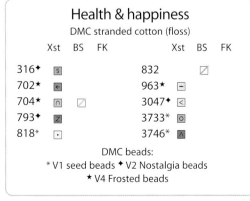

Wedding – Bride

This beautiful bride with her beaded dress in shades of lemon and cream will make a wonderful keepsake for the happy couple

❖ White linen, 32 count 15 x 11cm (6 x 4³/₈in)
❖ DMC stranded cotton (floss) as listed in the key
❖ Pink and yellow seed beads
❖ Tapestry needle, No 26
❖ White card with a 12.2 x 8.2cm (4⁷/₈ x 3¹/₄in) arched shaped opening

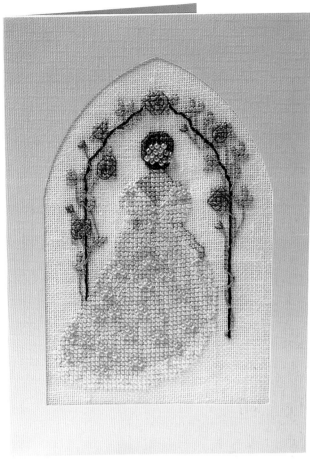

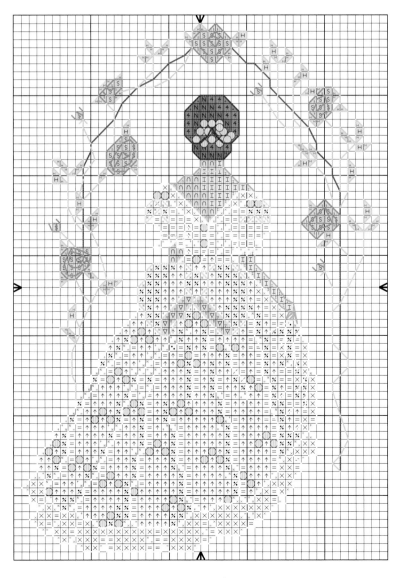

Bride
DMC stranded cotton (floss)

	Xst	BS	FK		Xst	BS	FK
335		☑		754	n		
356	N	☑		758		☑	
413		☑		776	S		▦**
563		☑		948	I		
564	H			3778	4		
744	▽	☑	▦*	3823	↑		
745	⅍	☐		3865	✕		
746	=						

DMC seed beads: * V1-06-744 pale tangerine
** V1-01-776 salmon pink

DESIGN SIZE: 10.5 x 7.4cm (4¹/₈ x 2⁷/₈in)
NOTE: each stitch on the chart is worked over two threads of linen. The seed beads are stitched on to the design in the positions marked on the chart with pink and yellow dots. The backstitch for the flower stems and the arch is stitched using two strands of stranded cotton (floss). Use the trace on page 109, and the finishing instructions on page 102 to cut the arch shaped card mount. A matching tag can be found on page 51.

Bride designed by Susan Penny

Anniversary cake

Whether they have been married for 2 or 20 years there's a couple who are sure to appreciate this anniversary card

❖ Cream evenweave, 28 count 15 x 11cm (6 x 4⅜in)
❖ DMC stranded cotton (floss) as listed in the key
❖ Tapestry needle, No 26
❖ Peach card with a 11.3 x 9.1cm (4½ x 3⅝in) oval opening

DESIGN SIZE: 9 x 8cm (3½ x 3⅛in).
NOTE: each stitch on the chart is worked over two threads of evenweave. The words and the french knots are worked in two strands of stranded cotton. Use the numbers chart on page 98 to add a year to the top of the cake.

Anniversary cake designed by Susan Penny

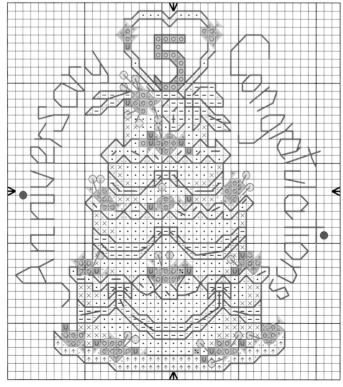

Anniversary cake
DMC stranded cotton (floss)

	Xst	BS	FK
Blanc	·		
Ecru	↑		
553		⊘	
554			▥
704	⊠		
3021		⊘	●
3340	U	⊘	
3341	○		
3823	−		
3865	⊠		

Golden wedding anniversary

For yourself or for some dear friends who are celebrating 25 or 50 years of marriage, a hand-stitched card is a wonderful keepsake of happy times together

❖ White evenweave, 30 count 15 x 11cm (6 x 4⅜in)
❖ DMC stranded cotton (floss) as listed in the key
❖ Gold metallic thread
❖ Tapestry needle, No 26
❖ Gold card with a 8 x 8cm (3⅛ x 3⅛in) heart shaped opening

DESIGN SIZE: 4.5 x 4.5cm (1¾ x 1¾in)
NOTE: each stitch on the chart is worked over two threads of evenweave. Use two strands of gold metallic for the cross stitch and backstitch. Use the trace on page 109, and the instructions on page 102 to cut a heart shaped mount.

Golden wedding designed by Claire Crompton

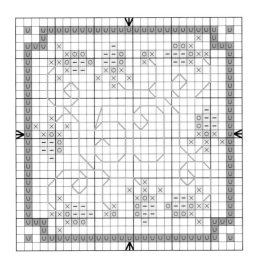

Golden wedding
DMC stranded cotton (floss)

	Xst	BS	FK
472	⊠		
3820	⊙		
3822	⊟		
Gold*	U	⧄	

* DMC divisible metallic gold thread

Silver wedding anniversary

❖ White evenweave, 28 count 15 x 11cm (6 x 4⅜in)
❖ DMC stranded cotton (floss) as listed in the key
❖ Silver metallic thread
❖ Tapestry needle, No 26
❖ White card with a 10 x 8cm (4 x 3⅛in) oval opening and silver decoration

DESIGN SIZE: 7 x 7cm (2¾ x 2¾in)
NOTE: each stitch on the chart is worked over two threads of evenweave. Use two strands of silver metallic for the cross stitch and the backstitch. The silver wedding card is shown stitched on page 42. A matching tag can be found on page 51.

Silver wedding designed by Claire Crompton

Silver wedding
DMC stranded cotton (floss)

	Xst	BS	FK
156	⊙		
157	U		
158	■		
762	+		
939		⧄	
Silver*	▨	⧄	

* DMC divisible metallic silver thread

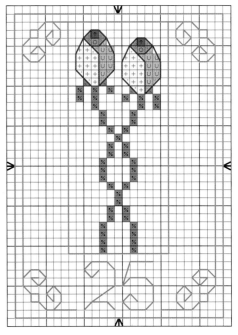

Ruby wedding anniversary

Notable anniversaries call for notable cards. Seed beads and backstitch give these cards a really individual look

❖ Cream linen, 26 count 20 x 15cm (8 x 6in)
❖ DMC stranded cotton (floss) as listed in the key
❖ Red seed beads
❖ Tapestry needle, No 26
❖ Red card with a 15 x 11cm (6 x 4⅜in)
   oval opening

DESIGN SIZE: will fit any card shape or size.
NOTE: each stitch on the chart is worked over four threads of linen. Use three strands of stranded cotton for the cross stitch and the backstitch. The red seed beads are stitched on to the design in the positions marked on the chart with red dots. Use the numbers chart on page 98 to add the dates to the design.

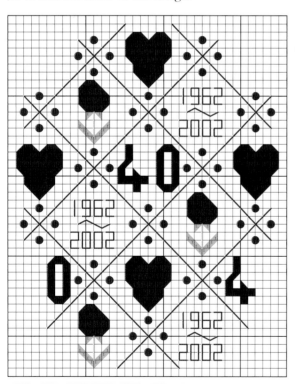

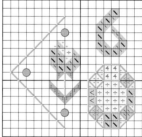

Diamond wedding anniversary

❖ Ivory evenweave, 28 count 11 x 9cm (4⅜ x 3½in)
❖ DMC stranded cotton (floss) as listed in the key
❖ Yellow seed beads
❖ Tapestry needle, No 26
❖ Ivory card with a 6.2 x 6.2cm (2½ x 2½in)
   heart shaped opening

DESIGN SIZE: will fit any card shape or size.
NOTE: each stitch on the chart is worked over two threads of evenweave. Use the ruby wedding chart (above left), replacing the hearts with the diamond shapes on the smaller chart (above). Use two strands of stranded cotton to backstitch the quilted lines. The yellow seed beads are stitched on to the design in the positions marked on the chart with red dots. Use the numbers chart on page 98 to add the dates to the design. Diamond wedding can be seen stitched on page 42. A matching tag can be found on page 51.

Ruby and Diamond wedding designed by Susan Penny

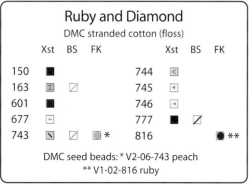

Ruby and Diamond
DMC stranded cotton (floss)

	Xst	BS	FK		Xst	BS	FK
150	■			744	◁		
163	Ⅰ	◹		745	⊞		
601	■			746	▷		
677	⊡			777	■	◹	
743	◩	◹	◉ *	816			◉ **

DMC seed beads: * V2-06-743 peach
** V1-02-816 ruby

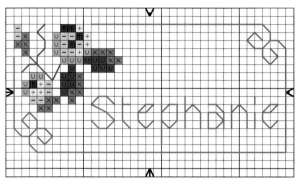

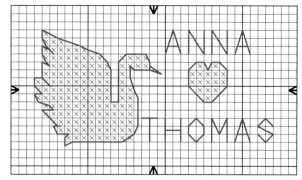

Valentine's day
DMC stranded cotton (floss)

	Xst	BS	FK
793	⬆		
962	⊠		
3052	⊡		
3607	▨		

The Valentine's day tag can be seen stitched with its matching card on page 43. The card chart can be found on page 44. Designed by Helen Philipps.

The swans place setting can be seen stitched with its matching card on page 43. The card chart can be found on page 45, and the alphabet for this design on page 98. Designed by Lesley Teare.

Swans
DMC stranded cotton (floss)

	Xst	BS	FK
5200	⊠		
Gold*		⊿	

*DMC antique gold 273

The health and happiness place setting can be seen stitched with its matching card on page 42. The card chart can be found on page 46, and the alphabet for this design on page 98. Designed by Claire Crompton.

Health & happiness
DMC stranded cotton (floss)

	Xst	BS	FK
151	⊟		
818	⊞		
832		⊿	
904	⊡	⊿	
988	⊠		
3733	⊡		
3803	▥		

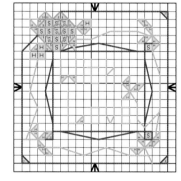

Bride
DMC stranded cotton (floss)

	Xst	BS	FK
413		⊿	
563		⊿	
564	⊞		
776	⊡		
3716		⊿	

The bride tag can be seen stitched with its matching card on page 42. The card chart can be found on page 47. Designed by Susan Penny.

Turn to the matching card chart pages for details of the fabric used in making these tags. General finishing instructions can be found on page 102.

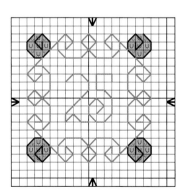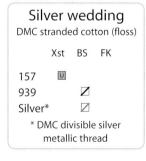

Silver wedding
DMC stranded cotton (floss)

	Xst	BS	FK
157	⊡		
939		⊿	
Silver*		⊿	

*DMC divisible silver metallic thread

The silver wedding tag can be seen stitched with its matching card on page 42. The card chart can be found on page 49. Designed by Claire Crompton.

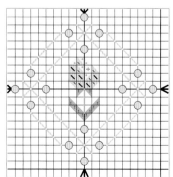

Diamond wedding
DMC stranded cotton (floss)

	Xst	BS	FK	
163	⊡	⊿		
677	⊞			
743	◩	⊿	▥	*

DMC seed beads: *
V2-06-743 peach

The diamond wedding tag can be seen stitched with its matching card on page 42. The card chart can be found on page 50. Designed by Susan Penny.

The Year's Special Days

Wherever you live in the world, and whatever your religion, there are days in the year that are unique and special to you, your family, and your friends. This chapter celebrates these occasions with distinctive designs inspired by different beliefs and countries of the world. If you know someone who celebrates the Chinese New Year then they will love the fiery dragon; Americans will enjoy the 4th of July red, white and blue; and the four leaf clover on the St Patrick's day card is sure to bring luck. So this year send an individual hand-stitched card with your love and best wishes for a happy day.

The Year's Special Days collection clockwise from top left – New Year, page 54; Flower basket, page 60; New car, page 61; Chinese New Year, page 55; Easter rabbit, page 58; Halloween pumpkin, page 62. Tags and place settings can be found on page 65.

New Year

Send good wishes in traditional style with this jolly Scotsman

❖ White evenweave, 28 count 20 x 15cm (8 x 6in)
❖ DMC stranded cotton (floss) as listed in the key
❖ Tapestry needle, No 26
❖ Green card with a 10cm (4in) diameter circular opening
❖ Tartan bow and ribbon
❖ Gold metallic pen

DESIGN SIZE: 8 x 6.3cm (3¼ x 2½in)
NOTE: each stitch on the chart is worked over two threads of evenweave. Use the gold metallic pen to draw a line around the opening cut in the card. Decorate the card with a strip of tartan ribbon and a bow across the bottom. A matching tag can be found on page 65.

New Year designed by Leslie Teare

New Year
DMC stranded cotton (floss)

	Xst	BS	FK
Blanc	·		
310	■	⁄	
347	▧		
350	⊞	⁄	
352	✓		
413	▦		
680	+		
701	U	⁄	
704	=		
951	⁒		
954	O		
3746	I		
3820	H		

Chinese New Year

This fiery dragon is an important symbol for the Chinese – a bringer of good luck and unity

❖ Pale green Aida, 14 count 18 x 15cm (7 x 6in)
❖ DMC stranded cotton (floss) as listed in the key
❖ Gold metallic thread
❖ Black seed beads
❖ Tapestry needle, No 24
❖ Green card with a 10 x 10cm (4 x 4in) square opening
❖ Gold metallic pen

DESIGN SIZE: 8.2 x 9.4cm (3¼ x 3¾in)
NOTE: use two strands of stranded cotton (floss) to backstitch the lettering. Sew the black seed beads on to the stitching in the positions marked on the chart with black dots. Draw a line around the opening cut in the card with a gold metallic pen. A matching tag can be found on page 65.

Chinese New Year designed by Julie Cook

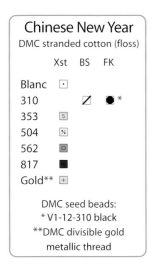

Chinese New Year
DMC stranded cotton (floss)

	Xst	BS	FK
Blanc	·		
310		╱	●*
353	S		
504	⅔		
562	◎		
817	■		
Gold**	⊞		

DMC seed beads:
* V1-12-310 black
**DMC divisible gold metallic thread

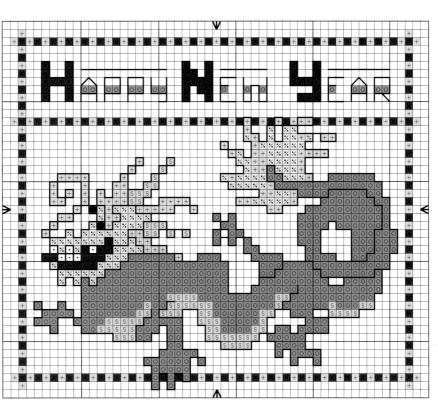

4th of July

A great day for the USA – send this card to celebrate American Independence Day

❖ Cream linen, 28 count 20 x 15cm (8 x 6in)
❖ DMC stranded cotton (floss) as listed in the key
❖ Tapestry needle, No 26
❖ Red card with a 10 x 10cm (4 x 4in) square opening
❖ Blue sticky-backed stationery stars
❖ Gold metallic pen

DESIGN SIZE: 7 x 8.5cm (2¾ x 3⅜in)
NOTE: each stitch on the chart is worked over two threads of linen. Use the gold metallic pen to draw a line around the opening cut in the card. Glue the blue stars across the bottom of the card.

4th of July designed by Helen Philipps

4th of July
DMC stranded cotton (floss)

	Xst	BS	FK
Blanc		◪	⬭
347	▨		
729	◉		
796	▦	◪	

Hanukkah

Celebrate the Jewish festival of lights with this colourful Hanukkah card

❖ White Aida, 14 count 15 x 10cm (6 x 4in)
❖ DMC stranded cotton (floss) as listed in the key
❖ Tapestry needle, No 24
❖ Mauve card with a 9.2 x 7.3cm (3⅝ x 2⅞in) rectangular opening
❖ Mauve cardboard

DESIGN SIZE: 8.8 x 6.8cm (3½ x 2⅝in)
NOTE: use the trace on page 109 to cut two triangles from the extra mauve card. Glue one along the top edge of the card and one on the bottom.

Hanukkah designed by Maria Diaz

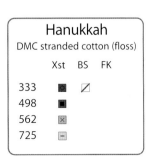

Hanukkah			
DMC stranded cotton (floss)			
	Xst	BS	FK
333	■	∕	
498	■		
562	⊠		
725	⊟		

Easter rabbit

Easter is the most important celebration in the Church year, when Christians reflect on days past, and look forward to the new year ahead

❖ Ivory linen, 30 count 15 x 11cm (6 x 4⅜in)
❖ DMC stranded cotton (floss) as listed in the key
❖ Tapestry needle, No 26
❖ Yellow card with a 12 x 8.5cm (4¾ x 3⅜in) rectangular opening

DESIGN SIZE: 10.7 x 7.5cm (4⅛ x 3in)
NOTE: each stitch on the chart is worked over two threads of linen. Use two strands of stranded cotton (floss) to backstitch the lettering. A matching tag can be found on page 65.

Easter rabbit designed by Julie Cook

Easter rabbit
DMC stranded cotton (floss)

	Xst	BS	FK
Blanc		◩	
422	⊠		
469		◪	
471	P		
472	Z		
610	◢		
611	⊡		
612	H		
726	+	◪	
743	▽		
783		◪	◙
833	‖		
839		◪	
3031	▲	◪	
3045	↑		
3078	○		

Easter flowers

Send your good wishes at Easter with these pretty spring flowers decorated with real pressed flower petals

❖ Cream linen, 28 count 15 x 11cm (6 x 4⅜in)
❖ DMC stranded cotton (floss) as listed in the key
❖ Tapestry needle, No 26
❖ Cream card with a 11 x 7cm (4⅜ x 2¾in) rectangular opening
❖ Pressed flower petals

DESIGN SIZE: 8.4 x 6.3cm (3⅜ x 2½in)
NOTE: each stitch on the chart is worked over two threads of linen. Decorate the card mount with pressed flower petals.

Easter flowers designed by Helen Philipps

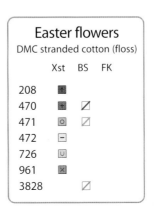

Easter flowers
DMC stranded cotton (floss)

	Xst	BS	FK
208	◼		
470	✚	⁄	
471	◎	⁄	
472	−		
726	U		
961	✖		
3828		⁄	

Mother's day – Mum

Show your mum that you care on Mother's day by sending her a hand-stitched card

❖ White hardanger, 22 count 12 x 10.5cm (4¾ x 4⅛in)
❖ DMC stranded cotton (floss) as listed in the key
❖ Tapestry needle, No 26
❖ Mauve card with a 7.5cm (3in) diameter circular opening

DESIGN SIZE: 7 x 7cm (2¾ x 2¾in)
NOTE: each stitch on the chart is worked over two threads of hardanger. Use two strands of stranded cotton (floss) for all the backstitch.

Mum designed by Claire Crompton

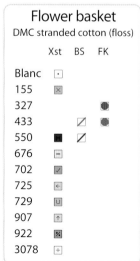

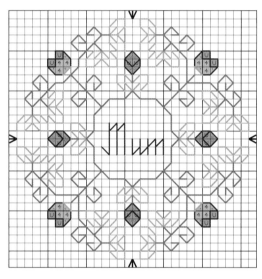

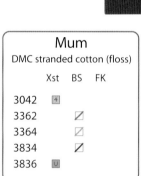

Mum
DMC stranded cotton (floss)

	Xst	BS	FK
3042	4		
3362		☑	
3364		☑	
3834		☑	
3836	U		

Flower basket

❖ White evenweave, 28 count 15 x 10cm (6 x 4in)
❖ DMC stranded cotton (floss) as listed in the key
❖ Tapestry needle, No 26
❖ Green card with a 7.5 x 5.5cm (3 x 2¼in) rectangular opening

DESIGN SIZE: 6.25 x 4.8cm (2½ x 1⅞in)
NOTE: each stitch on the chart is worked over two threads of evenweave. The flower basket is shown stitched on page 52. A matching tag can be found on page 65.

Flower basket designed by Lesley Teare

Flower basket
DMC stranded cotton (floss)

	Xst	BS	FK
Blanc	·		
155	☒		
327			●
433		☑	●
550	■	☑	
676	−		
702	☑		
725	←		
729	U		
907	↑		
922	☒		
3078	+		

Father's day – Sport

Whether your dad is the sporty type or he just dreams of a sporty car, then one of these cards is sure to please

❖ Cream evenweave, 28 count 11 x 9cm (4³⁄₈ x 3½in)
❖ DMC stranded cotton (floss) as listed in the key
❖ Tapestry needle, No 26
❖ Green card with a 7 x 5cm (2³⁄₄ x 2in) rectangular opening
❖ Gold metallic pen

DESIGN SIZE: 6.75 x 5cm (2⅝ x 2in)
NOTE: each stitch on the card is worked over two threads of evenweave. Use the gold metallic pen to draw a line around the opening cut in the card.

Sport designed by Mari Richards

New car

❖ White Aida, 14 count 15 x 11cm (6 x 4³⁄₈in)
❖ DMC stranded cotton (floss) as listed in the key
❖ Silver metallic thread
❖ Tapestry needle, No 24
❖ Pale blue card with a 7.5 x 7.5cm (3 x 3in) square opening

DESIGN SIZE: 5.2 x 7cm (2⅛ x 2³⁄₄in)
NOTE: use three strands of stranded cotton (floss) for the backstitch, and one strand of silver to backstitch the car lights and front grill. The silver cross stitch is worked using two strands of silver plus one strand of DMC stranded cotton (floss) in 415 grey. The new car can be seen stitched on page 53. A matching tag can be found on page 65.

New car designed by Maria Diaz

Sport
DMC stranded cotton (floss)

	Xst	BS	FK
Blanc	·		
310	■	◿	
318		◿	
420	◪		
422	↑	◿	▣
666	▦		
726	✕		
869		◿	
986		◿	
988	N		
3801	U		
3828	I		

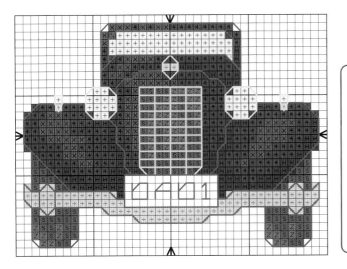

New car
DMC stranded cotton (floss)

	Xst	BS	FK		Xst	BS	FK
350	✕			817	✚		
413	▧			3799		◿	
414	◿			Silver**			▢
498	▦			Blend*			⊞
747	⊞						

*DMC divisible silver + 415
**DMC divisible silver metallic thread

Halloween – Ghost

If you know someone who celebrates halloween, they are sure to love the happy ghost or pumpkin card

❖ White Aida, 14 count 9.4 x 11cm (3¾ x 4⅜in)
❖ DMC stranded cotton (floss) as listed in the key
❖ Tapestry needle, No 24
❖ Burgundy card with a 5.6 x 8cm (2¼ x 3⅛in) rectangular opening

DESIGN SIZE: 5.1 x 7cm (2 x 2¾in)
NOTE: use two strands of stranded cotton (floss) to work the backstitch.

Ghost designed by Sam Hawkins

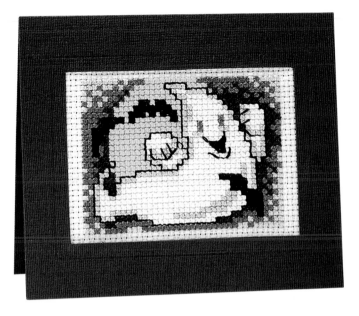

Ghost
DMC stranded cotton (floss)

	Xst	BS	FK
Blanc	·		
307	U		
310	■	╱	
826	↑		
3865	■		
3687	▨		
3689	+		
3841	–		

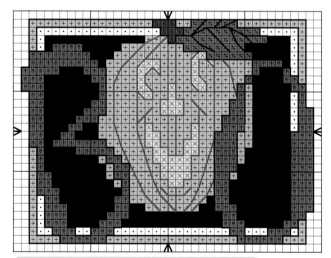

Pumpkin
DMC stranded cotton (floss)

	Xst	BS	FK		Xst	BS	FK
Blanc	·			742	+		
310	■	╱		947	↑		
434	▨	╱		973	⊠		
470	▨						

Pumpkin

❖ White Aida, 14 count 10.5 x 15cm (4⅛ x 6in)
❖ DMC stranded cotton (floss) as listed in the key
❖ Tapestry needle, No 24
❖ Black card with a 6 x 8cm (2⅜ x 3⅛in) rectangular opening
❖ Orange card for pumpkin shape
❖ Gold metallic pen

DESIGN SIZE: 5.7 x 7.5cm (2¼ x 3in)
NOTE: use two strands of stranded cotton (floss) to work the backstitch. Use the gold metallic pen to draw a line around the opening cut in the card. Use the shape on page 109 to cut a pumpkin from orange card, then glue it to the front of the card. The pumpkin card can be seen stitched on page 52. A matching tag can be found on page 65.

Pumpkin designed by Sam Hawkins

Thanksgiving

*Celebrate this American national holiday with a
special card to give thanks for a successful harvest*

❖ Biscuit Belfast linen, 32 count 15 x 11cm (6 x 4⅜in)
❖ DMC stranded cotton (floss) as listed in the key
❖ Tapestry needle, No 26
❖ Beige card with a 11 x 7cm (4⅜ x 2¾in)
   rectangular opening

DESIGN SIZE: 7.5 x 5.7cm (3 x 2¼in)
NOTE: each stitch on the chart is worked over two
threads of linen. The backstitch lettering and french
knots are worked using two strands of stranded
cotton (floss).

Thanksgiving designed by Sam Hawkins

Thanksgiving
DMC stranded cotton (floss)

	Xst	BS	FK
310	■	◪	
435	S	◪	
470	I		
720		◪	◉
722	▽		
739	⊠		
754	▤		
783	▨		
801	★		◉
3326	▨		

St Patrick's day

Celebrate the luck of the Irish and stitch this St Patrick's day card

❖ Antique white linen, 28 count 10.5 x 13cm (4⅛ x 5¼in)
❖ DMC stranded cotton (floss) as listed in the key
❖ Tapestry needle, No 26
❖ Green card with a 7.4 x 9.5cm (2⅞ x 3¾in) rectangular opening

DESIGN SIZE: 6 x 8.2cm (2⅜ x 3¼in)
NOTE: each stitch on the chart is worked over two threads of linen.

St Patrick's day designed by Helen Philipps

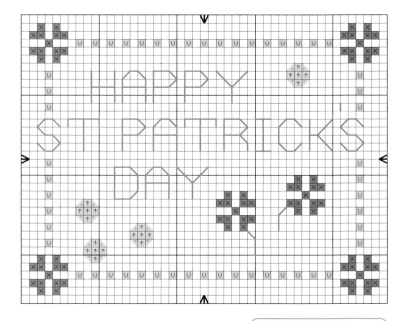

St Patrick's day
DMC stranded cotton (floss)

	Xst	BS	FK
701	☒	◩	
704	Ⓤ		
3820	↑		

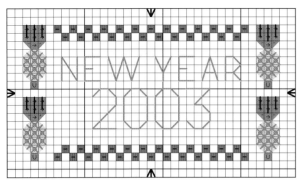

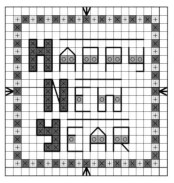

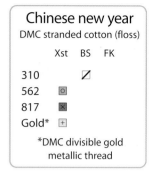

The new year place setting can be seen stitched with its matching card on page 52. The card chart can be found on page 54, and the alphabet on page 98. Designed by Lesley Teare.

New year
DMC stranded cotton (floss)

	Xst	BS	FK
310		◪	
350	⊞		
701	Ụ	◪	
704	═		
954	◌		
3746	➡		

Happy Easter
DMC stranded cotton (floss)

	Xst	BS	FK
469		◪	
471	P		
726	⊞	◪	
3078	◌		

The happy Easter tag can be seen stitched with its matching card on page 52. The card chart can be found on page 58. Designed by Julie Cook.

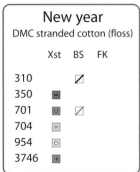

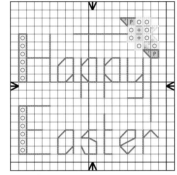

Turn to the matching card chart pages for details of the fabric used in making these tags. General finishing instructions can be found on page 102.

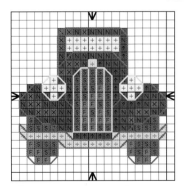

New car
DMC stranded cotton (floss)

	Xst	BS	FK
350	☒		
413	▨		
414	F		
498	◪		
747	⊞		
817	N		
3799		◪	
Silver*	▱		
Blend**	⊞		

*DMC divisible silver metallic thread
**415 + DMC divisible silver metallic thread

The new car tag can be seen stitched with its matching card on page 53. The card chart can be found on page 61. Designed by Maria Diaz.

The Chinese new year tag can be seen stitched with its matching card on page 52. The card chart can be found on page 55. Designed by Julie Cook.

Chinese new year
DMC stranded cotton (floss)

	Xst	BS	FK
310		◪	
562	◌		
817	☒		
Gold*	⊞		

*DMC divisible gold metallic thread

Flower basket
DMC stranded cotton (floss)

	Xst	BS	FK
Blanc	·		
155	☒		
433		◪	
550	▪	◪	
702	✓		
725	Ụ		
907	↑		
922	▨		
3078	⊞		

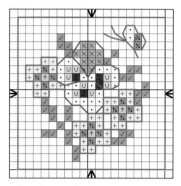

The flower basket tag can be seen stitched with its matching card on page 52. The card chart can be found on page 60. Designed by Lesley Teare.

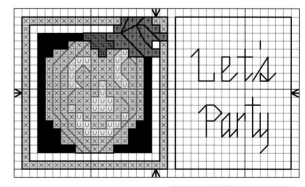

The pumpkin place setting can be seen stitched with its matching card on page 52. The card chart can be found on page 62. Designed by Sam Hawkins.

Pumpkin
DMC stranded cotton (floss)

	Xst	BS	FK
310	▪	◪	
434	▨	◪	
470	▨		
742	☒		
973	Ụ		

Happy Christmas

Christmas
2002
HARRIET

For you

Christmas

We all love to stitch for Christmas, so on the next few pages you will find a wonderful selection of traditional, whimsical and religious card designs. There are plenty of fun designs of jolly Santas, happy penguins and cute angels; traditional designs of Christmas trees and robins; religious design of the nativity; and designs that fit shaped cards like a stocking or arch. Some of the designs are on Aida, others are on finer fabric like evenweave and linen. To complement some of the designs there are matching tags and party place settings, that can be personalized using the alphabets provided. What nicer way to say Merry Christmas than with a unique hand-stitched card.

Christmas collection clockwise from top left – Happy Santa, page 68; Christmas woodland, page 76; Penguin, page 80; Christmas window, page 75; Christmas girl, page 71; Santa heart, page 69. Tags and place settings can be found on page 83.

Santa wreath

This Santa wreath is a great way to wish your friends or family a happy Christmas

❖ White Aida, 14 count 13 x 11cm (5¼ x 4⅜in)
❖ DMC stranded cotton (floss) as listed in the key
❖ Tapestry needle, No 24
❖ Red card with a 8cm (3⅛in) diameter circular opening
❖ Silver flat-backed faceted stars

DESIGN SIZE: 7.3 x 7cm (2⅞ x 2¾in)
NOTE: glue a silver star on to each corner of the card.

Santa wreath designed by Sam Hawkins

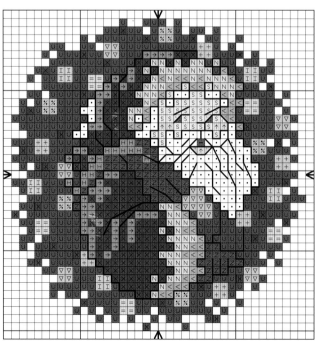

Santa wreath
DMC stranded cotton (floss)

	Xst	BS	FK
Blanc	·		
321	▨		
413	▨	◿	
554	+		
699	U		
726	=		
776	↑		
813	✕		
907	▽		
948	S		
3046	<		
3047	N		
3705	→		
3716	I		
3862	▨		
3864	H		

Santa heart

Send your love to the special person in your life, and to wish them the best for the Christmas holidays

❖ White Aida, 14 count 11.3 x 17.8cm (4½ x 7in)
❖ DMC stranded cotton (floss) as listed in the key
❖ Tapestry needle, No 24
❖ White card with a 7.4 x 8.8cm (2⅞ x 3½in) shaped opening
❖ Wooden heart shaped buttons

DESIGN SIZE: 7.1 x 8.8cm (2¾ x 3½in)
NOTE: use two strands of red stranded cotton (floss) to backstitch the grid lines and heart shape. Sew the heart shaped buttons on to the Aida either side of the design. Use the trace on page 109 and the finishing instructions on page 102, to cut a shaped card mount. A matching tag can be found on page 83.

Santa heart designed by Sam Hawkins

Santa heart			
DMC stranded cotton (floss)			
	Xst	BS	FK
Blanc	·		
310	■	╱	
321	▦	╱	
413		╱	
632		╱	
700	s		
758	+		
762	→		
776	=		
948	U		
3705	✕		
3773	↑		
3774	⁒		

Happy Santa

Send your best wishes and love with this happy Santa design

❖ White Aida, 14 count 12 x 10cm (4¾ x 4in)
❖ DMC stranded cotton (floss) as listed in the key
❖ Tapestry needle, No 24
❖ Red card with gold printed Happy Christmas – no opening

DESIGN SIZE: 9 x 7cm (3⅝ x 2¾in)
NOTE: use two strands of stranded cotton (floss) for the backstitch and french knots. Fray the edges of the fabric by removing two rows of Aida on all sides of the design. Use double sided tape to attach the stitching to the front of the card. A matching tag can be found on page 83.

Happy Santa designed by Sam Hawkins

Happy Santa
DMC stranded cotton (floss)

	Xst	BS	FK
Blanc	·		
310	■	▨	●
414	Y		
666	▨		◐
700	◎		
712	↑		
776	−		
783	U		
816	S		
948	=		
957	<		
3840	+		

Christmas – Angel

Let this cute angel or Victorian girl carry the Christmas message to someone special this year

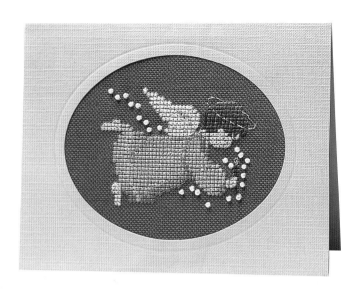

- ❖ Wedgwood blue linen, 28 count 11 x 14.4cm (4⅜ x 5¾in)
- ❖ DMC stranded cotton (floss) as listed in the key
- ❖ Gold metallic thread
- ❖ Pearl white seed beads
- ❖ Tapestry needle, No 26
- ❖ Pale blue card with a 8 x 10.3cm (3⅛ x 4⅛in) oval opening

DESIGN SIZE: 5.5 x 7.5cm (2¼ x 3in)
NOTE: each stitch on the chart is worked over two threads of linen. Use one strand of gold metallic thread to backstitch the halo. The beads are stitched on to the design in the positions marked on the chart with a grey dot.

Christmas angel designed by Susan Penny

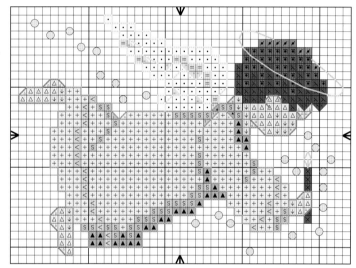

Christmas angel
DMC stranded cotton (floss)

	Xst	BS	FK		Xst	BS	FK
Blanc	·		▣ *	800	⊞		
356		◪		809	⑤		
666	✖			920	◪		
676	◁			921	▣		
754	↓			922	◪		
758	∨			948	△		
778	⊟		◩	961			◪
799	▲			Gold**			◪

*DMC seed beads: V1-10-Blanc
**DMC divisible gold metallic thread

Girl

- ❖ Cream Aida, 14 count 11.5 x 9cm (4½ x 3½in)
- ❖ DMC stranded cotton (floss) as listed in the key
- ❖ Tapestry needle, No 24
- ❖ Red card with a 7 x 5cm (2¾ x 2in) rectangular opening
- ❖ Gold metallic pen

DESIGN SIZE: 7 x 4.5cm (2¾ x 1¾in)
NOTE: use the gold metallic pen to draw a line around the card opening. Christmas girl can be seen stitched on page 66. A matching tag can be found on page 83.

Christmas girl designed by Sue Cook

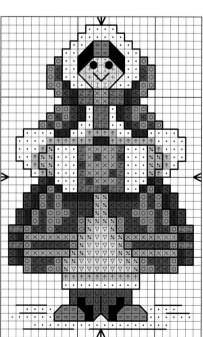

Christmas girl
DMC stranded cotton (floss)

	Xst	BS	FK
Blanc	·		
340	✖		
351	○		
353	＋		
433	▣		
435	▤		
452	↑		
742	⅔		
744	▽		
815	▣		
817	▣		
838	■	◪	●
948	⊺		
3746	▨		

Nativity

Bethlehem is where the Christmas story began, and this card evokes the spirit of the holy city

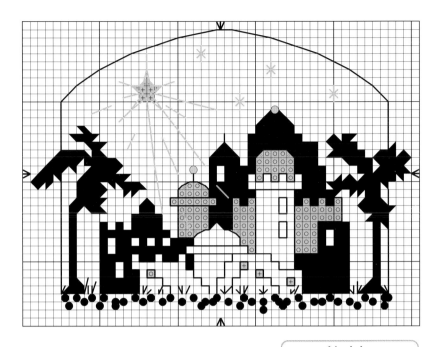

❖ Cream evenweave, 27 count 10 x 15cm (4 x 6in)
❖ DMC stranded cotton (floss) as listed in the key
❖ Tapestry needle, No 26
❖ Gold card with a 7.7 x 11.5cm (3 x 4½in) shaped opening

DESIGN SIZE: 7 x 9.8cm (2¾ x 3⅞in)
NOTE: each stitch on the chart is worked over two threads of evenweave. The shaped backstitch border line and french knots are worked in two strands of black stranded cotton (floss). Use the trace on page 110, and the finishing instructions on page 102 to cut the arch shaped card mount.

Nativity designed by Susan Penny

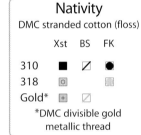

Nativity
DMC stranded cotton (floss)

	Xst	BS	FK
310	■	◿	●
318	◉		▦
Gold*	✚	◿	

*DMC divisible gold metallic thread

Topiary Christmas

*This traditional Christmas greeting, finished
with a single star charm, has extra warmth
when stitched on natural linen*

❖ Natural linen, 28 count 15 x 11cm (6 x 4⅜in)
❖ DMC stranded cotton (floss) as listed in the key
❖ Silver star-shaped charm
❖ Tapestry needle, No 26
❖ Cream card with a 11 x 7.3cm (4⅜ x 3in)
   rectangular opening

DESIGN SIZE: 9 x 7.3cm (3½ x 3in)
NOTE: each stitch on the chart is worked over two
threads of linen. Sew the star-shaped charm on to
the stitching in the position marked on the chart by
a black dot.

Topiary Christmas designed by Helen Philipps

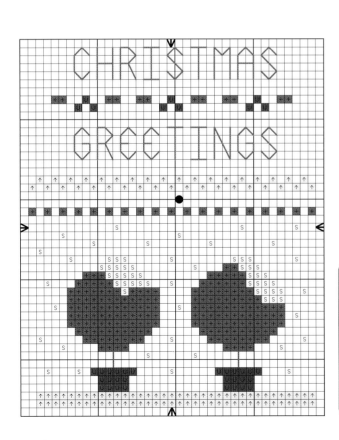

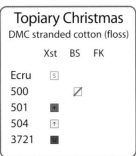

Topiary Christmas
DMC stranded cotton (floss)

	Xst	BS	FK
Ecru	S		
500		◿	
501	■		
504	↑		
3721	▥		

Christmas stocking

We all love a stocking full of goodies at Christmas. This one decorated with angels is sure to bring joy to the recipient

❖ Navy Aida, 14 count 15 x 11cm (6 x 4⅜in)
❖ DMC stranded cotton (floss) as listed in the key
❖ Silver metallic thread
❖ Tapestry needle, No 24
❖ Blue card with a 11.5 x 8cm (4½ x 3⅛in) stocking shaped opening

DESIGN SIZE: 11.5 x 8cm (4½ x 3⅛in)
NOTE: work the silver backstitch using three strands and the remainder in two strands of stranded cotton (floss). Use the trace on page 110 to cut the stocking shape from the front of the blue card.

Christmas stocking designed by Maria Diaz

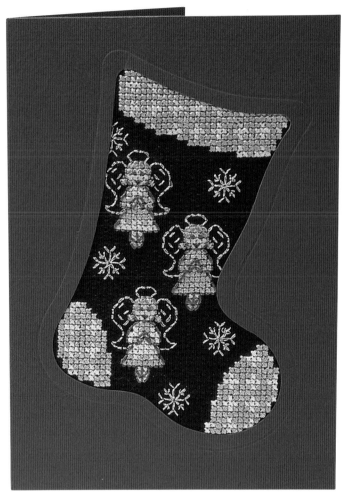

Christmas stocking
DMC stranded cotton (floss)

	Xst	BS	FK
Blanc	·		
211	▽		
349		∕	
729		∕	
744	⊡		
800	⊠		
931		∕	
948	⊟		
Silver*		∕	

*DMC divisible silver metallic thread

Christmas window

This Christmas, why not bring the message of peace to someone special with this beautiful stained glass window

❖ White Aida, 14 count 15 x 11cm (6 x 4⅜in)
❖ DMC stranded cotton (floss) as listed in the key
❖ Gold metallic thread
❖ Tapestry needle, No 24
❖ Gold card with a 11.5 x 6.5cm (4½ x 2⅝in) arch shaped opening

DESIGN SIZE: 11.5 x 6.5cm (4½ x 2⅝in)
NOTE: use two strands of gold metallic for the cross stitch and one strand for the backstitch. Cut an arch shaped opening in the front of the card using the trace on page 110. A matching tag can be found on page 83.

Christmas window designed by Claire Crompton

Christmas window

DMC stranded cotton (floss)

	Xst	BS	FK
168	✓		
309	✕		
498	Z		
550	■		
797	N		
799	◁		
820	S		
844	∧		
986	◎		
988	C		
3837	U		
3865	·		
Gold*	4		◻

*DMC divisible gold metallic thread

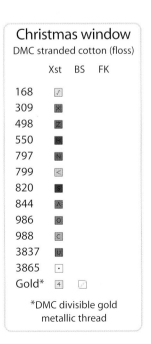

Christmas woodland

This cute fox and badger play happily as the snow falls on a winter woodland scene

❖ Black evenweave, 28 count 15 x 11cm (6 x 4⅜in)
❖ DMC stranded cotton (floss) as listed in the key
❖ Gold metallic thread
❖ Kreinek blending filament – colour 032
❖ Tapestry needle, No 26
❖ White card with a 11 x 7cm (4⅜ x 2¾in) arch shaped opening

DESIGN SIZE: 11 x 7cm (4⅜ x 2¾in)
NOTE: each stitch on the chart is worked over two threads on the fabric. Blend two strands of white stranded cotton (floss) with one strand of blending filament for the snow. The star is worked using two strands of gold metallic thread. The backstitch outline is worked using two strands of stranded cotton (floss). Use the trace on page 110 to cut an arch shaped opening in the front of the card. A matching tag can be found on page 83.

Christmas woodland designed by Julie Cook

Christmas woodland
DMC stranded cotton (floss)

	Xst	BS	FK		Xst	BS	FK
Blanc	·			758	=		
310	■	╱	●	782	N		
413				829	◈	╱	
414				975	▩		
415	I			3773	Z		
469	✕			Blend*	↑		
471	O			Gold**		╱	
746	−						

*Blend: 3865 + 032 Kreinek blending filament
**DMC divisible gold metallic thread

Christmas – Wreath

Wreaths are a traditional decoration at Christmas. Here are two, each with its own unique charm

❖ Cream evenweave, 28 count 15 x 11cm (6 x 4³⁄₈in)
❖ DMC stranded cotton (floss) as listed in the key
❖ Tapestry needle, No 26
❖ Yellow card with a 7.5 x 7.5cm (3 x 3in) square opening

DESIGN SIZE: 6 x 6cm (2³⁄₈ x 2³⁄₈in)
NOTE: each stitch on the chart is worked over two threads of evenweave fabric.

Christmas wreath designed by Susan Penny

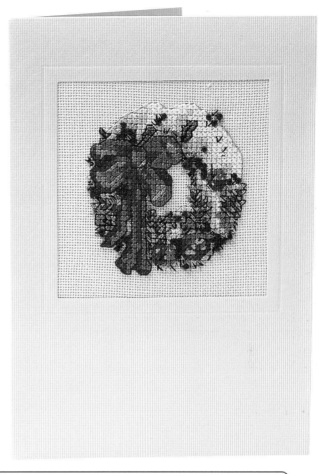

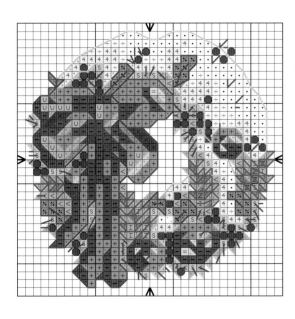

Christmas wreath
DMC stranded cotton (floss)

	Xst	BS	FK		Xst	BS	FK		Xst	BS	FK
Blanc	·			433		☑		989	◰		
349	▨			611	▨			3046	Ⅰ		
350	▦			817	▦	☑	●	3348	S		
351	+			828	4			3755			☑
352	U			895		☑		3756	÷		
353	▣			988	▨						

Singing robin

❖ White evenweave, 28 count 11.5 x 9cm (4½ x 3½in)
❖ DMC stranded cotton (floss) as listed in the key
❖ Tapestry needle, No 26
❖ Red card with a 6.5cm (2½in) diameter circular opening

DESIGN SIZE: 5.5 x 5.5cm (2¼ x 2¼in)
NOTE: each stitch on the chart is worked over two threads of evenweave fabric. The singing robin card is shown stitched on page 7.

Singing robin designed by Lesley Teare

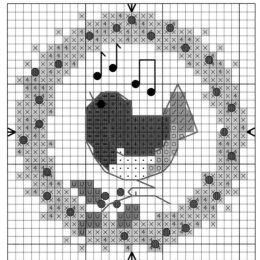

Singing robin
DMC stranded cotton (floss)

	Xst	BS	FK
Blanc	·		
310		☑	●
347			●
350	▦		
433	▨	☑	
434	▨		
701	U		
906	4		
907	×		
3046	◉		
3828	☑		

Pear tree

Stitch someone this unusual symbol of peace and love at Christmas, or send the blue tit for a more traditional greeting

❖ Cream linen, 28 count 15 x 11cm (6 x 4⅜in)
❖ DMC stranded cotton (floss) as listed in the key
❖ Gold metallic thread
❖ Gold seed beads
❖ Tapestry needle, No 26
❖ Yellow card with a 11.5 x 6.5cm (4½ x 2½in) arch shaped opening

DESIGN SIZE: 9.5 x 5.6cm (3¾ x 2¼in)
NOTE: each stitch on the chart is worked over two threads of linen. Stitch the dove, which is on a separate chart, above the pear tree. Backstitch the tree in one strand of gold metallic, the dove in two strands, and the lettering in two strands of stranded cotton (floss). Stitch the seed beads on to the design in the positions marked on the chart with yellow dots.

Pear tree and Snowy garden designed by Susan Penny

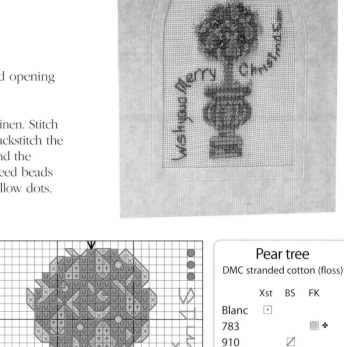

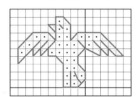

Snowy garden
DMC stranded cotton (floss)

	Xst	BS	FK		Xst	BS	FK
Blanc	·	☐	☐	932	▽		
310	■	◪	●	936		◪	
349	▨			945			
350	▦			951	▽		
433		◪		3752	↑		
828	④			3753	○		
895		◪		3755		◪	
931		◪	◕	3756	÷		

Pear tree
DMC stranded cotton (floss)

	Xst	BS	FK
Blanc	·		
783			▨ ❖
910		◪	
911	U		
993	✕		
3853	↑	◪	
Blend*			◕
Blend**		◪	
Gold◆		◪	

❖DMC seed beads:
V1-08-783 Gold
*910 + DMC Gold divisible metallic
**3853 + Gold divisible
◆Gold divisible

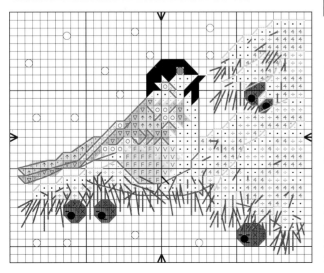

Snowy garden

❖ Grey evenweave, 28 count 9 x 12cm (3½ x 4⅝in)
❖ DMC stranded cotton (floss) as listed in the key
❖ White seed beads
❖ Tapestry needle, No 26
❖ Blue card with a 5.5 x 7cm (2¼ x 2¾in) rectangular opening
❖ Blue bow

DESIGN SIZE: 4.5 x 6cm (1¾ x 2⅜in)
NOTE: each stitch on the chart is worked over two threads of evenweave. Stitch the seed beads on to the design in the positions marked on the chart with cream dots. Glue the bow on to the card mount. Snowy garden is shown stitched on page 7.

Winter robin

This robin, with his bright red breast, evokes the spirit of early Christmas cards

❖ Blue Aida, 14 count 12.7 x 17.7cm (5 x 6in)
❖ DMC stranded cotton (floss) as listed in the key
❖ Tapestry needle, No 24
❖ White card with a 9 x 13cm (3⅝ x 5¼in) oval opening

DESIGN SIZE: 8.5 x 9cm (3⅜ x 3⅝in)
NOTE: use two strands of stranded cotton (floss) for the backstitch and french knots.

Winter robin designed by Julie Cook

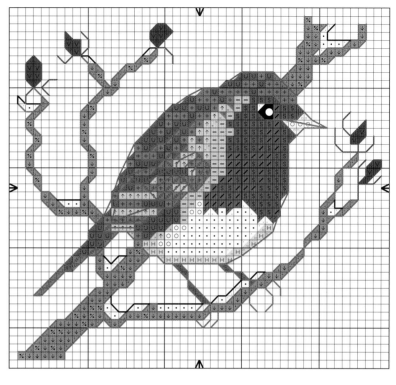

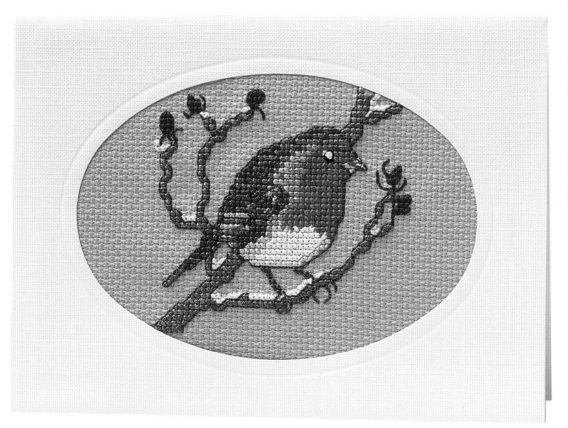

Winter robin			
DMC stranded cotton (floss)			
	Xst	BS	FK
Blanc	·	⧄	⬡
301	⑊		
310	■		
318	⊟		
371	▨		
535	▨	⧄	
611	↓		
720	▨		
762	○		
839	∪	⧄	
840	+		
842	↑		
3072	H		
3777	▨	⧄	

Snowman

Wrapped up warm in scarf and hat this fun snowman and penguin are great for sending Christmas greetings

❖ Blue Aida, 14 count 15 x 10.5cm (6 x 4⅛in)
❖ DMC stranded cotton (floss) as listed in the key
❖ Tapestry needle, No 24
❖ White card with a 7.5 x 5.7cm (3 x 2¼in) rectangular opening
❖ Silver metallic pen

Design Size: 7 x 5.2cm (2¾ x 2⅛in)
Note: work the backstitch in two strands of stranded cotton (floss). Use the silver metallic pen to draw a line around the opening cut in the card.

Snowman designed by Maria Diaz

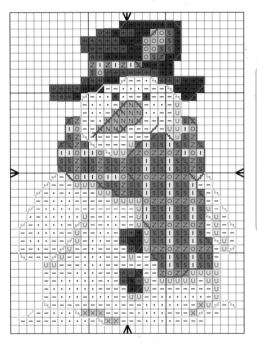

Snowman
DMC stranded cotton (floss)

	Xst	BS	FK		Xst	BS	FK
Blanc	·			932	=		
472	I			3752	N		
722	N			3756	✳	╱	
898	✳	╱		3777	▦		
910	S			3810	Z		
912	O			3830	↑		

Penguin

❖ Blue Aida, 14 count 15 x 11cm (6 x 4¼in)
❖ DMC stranded cotton (floss) as listed in the key
❖ Tapestry needle, No 24
❖ Blue card with a 7cm (2¾in) diameter circular opening

Design Size: 7 x 5.2cm (2¾ x 2⅛in)
Note: work the backstitch in two strands of stranded cotton (floss). Penguin is shown stitched on page 67. A matching tag can be found on page 83.

Penguin designed by Maria Diaz

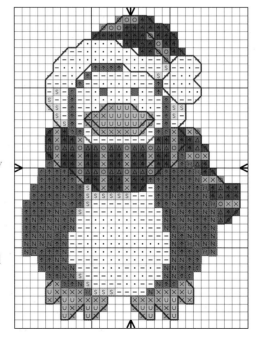

Penguin
DMC stranded cotton (floss)

	Xst	BS	FK
Blanc	·		
349	▦		
351	◎		
645	↑		
646	N		
814		╱	
844		╱	
970	✕		
972	U		
3607	▲		
3752	S		
3756	−		

Animal nativity

The cattle look down as baby Jesus sleeps.
Send the Christian message of Christmas with
this traditional nativity scene

❖ Beige evenweave, 28 count 15 x 11cm (6 x 4⅜in)
❖ DMC stranded cotton (floss) as listed in the key
❖ Gold metallic thread
❖ Tapestry needle, No 26
❖ Blue card with a 11 x 7.3cm (4⅜ x 2⅞in)
   rectangular opening

DESIGN SIZE: 9.2 x 7.5cm (3⅝ x 3in)
NOTE: each stitch on the chart is worked over two threads of
evenweave.

Animal nativity designed by Julie Cook

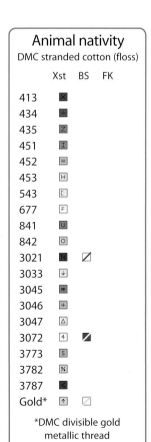

Animal nativity

DMC stranded cotton (floss)

	Xst	BS	FK
413	▨		
434	▨		
435	Z		
451	I		
452	=		
453	H		
543	C		
677	F		
841	U		
842	O		
3021	▨	◢	
3033	↓		
3045	▨		
3046	+		
3047	△		
3072	4	◢	
3773	S		
3782	⅜		
3787	▨		
Gold*	↑	◿	

*DMC divisible gold
metallic thread

Christmas tree

Send a bright and modern greeting this year. This Christmas tree has pink candy canes and silver trim and is topped with a pink star

❖ Navy Aida, 14 count 18 x 13cm (7 x 5¼in)
❖ DMC stranded cotton (floss) as listed in the key
❖ Silver metallic thread
❖ Tapestry needle, No 24
❖ White card with a 13 x 9cm (5¼ x 3½in) tree shaped opening
❖ Pink flat-backed faceted star

DESIGN SIZE: 13 x 9cm (5¼ x 3½in)
NOTE: blend two strands of the silver thread with one strand of DMC stranded cotton (floss) colour 3753 for the cross stitch and backstitch. Cut a tree shape from the front of the card using the trace on page 110. Glue the pink star on the card at the top of the tree.

Christmas tree designed by Maria Diaz

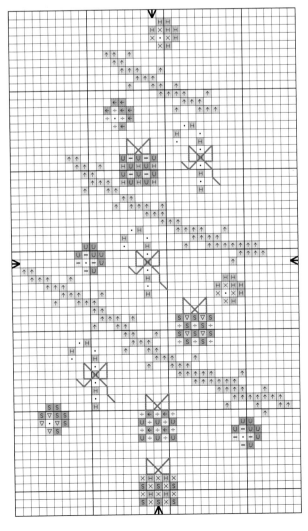

Christmas tree
DMC stranded cotton (floss)

	Xst	BS	FK
Blanc	·		
209	U		
211	−		
799	←		
800	÷		
894	H		
958	S		
963	⊠		
964	▽		
Blend*	↑	╱	

*DMC divisible silver metallic thread + 3753

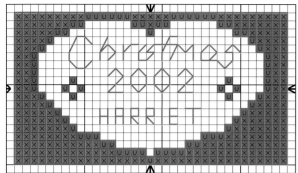

The Santa heart place setting can be seen stitched with its matching card on page 66. The card chart can be found on page 69, and the alphabet on page 98. Designed by Sam Hawkins.

Santa heart
DMC stranded cotton (floss)

	Xst	BS	FK
321	U	◪	
700	X		

Christmas girl
DMC stranded cotton (floss)

	Xst	BS	FK
Blanc	·		
340	H		
433	◪		
817	▣		
838		◪	◼
948	↑		

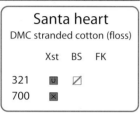

The Christmas girl tag can be seen stitched with its matching card on page 66. The card chart can be found on page 71. Designed by Sue Cook.

Turn to the matching card chart pages for details of the fabric used in making these tags. General finishing instructions can be found on page 102.

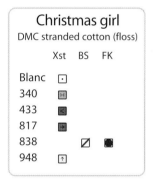

Christmas woodland
DMC stranded cotton (floss)

	Xst	BS	FK
Blanc	·		
310	◼	◪	
746	−		
758	=		
782	N		
975	S		
3773	Z		
Gold*	◪		

*DMC divisible gold metallic thread

The Christmas woodland tag can be seen stitched with its matching card on page 66. The card chart can be found on page 76. Designed by Julie Cook.

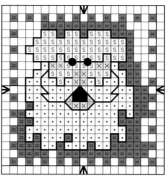

Happy Santa
DMC stranded cotton (floss)

	Xst	BS	FK
Blanc	·		
310	◼	◪	●
666	▦		
712	S		
776	X		

The happy Santa tag can be seen stitched with its matching card on page 66. The card chart can be found on page 70. Designed by Sam Hawkins.

Christmas window
DMC stranded cotton (floss)

	Xst	BS	FK
550	◪		
797	N		
820	◼		
3799	▩		
3837	U		
Gold*		◪	

*DMC divisible gold metallic thread

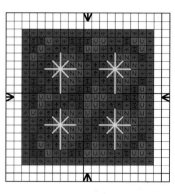

The Christmas window tag can be seen stitched with its matching card on page 67. The card chart can be found on page 75. Designed by Claire Crompton.

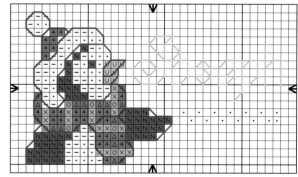

The penguin place setting can be seen stitched with its matching card on page 67. The card chart can be found on page 80, and the alphabet on page 98. Designed by Maria Diaz.

Penguin
DMC stranded cotton (floss)

	Xst	BS	FK
Blanc	·	◪	
349	◪		
351	O		
646	X		
814		◪	
844		◪	
970	X		
972	U		
3607	▲		
3756	−		

Special Wishes

Stitchers can always find time to sew a card for a special event, so this chapter is full of delightful designs that will get you rushing for your needle. Many different occasions have been covered, from passing the driving test to passing exams. There are designs for a new home, new job, moving away and retirement. Black cats for good luck, and an apple to wish someone a speedy recovery. Flowers to say thank you, or to say hello to a particular friend. To accompany some of the cards there are matching designs that can be used for gift tags and party place settings. So start stitching now, because it won't be long before you will be sending some special wishes again.

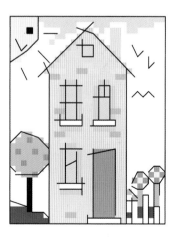

Special Wishes collection clockwise from top left – Bon voyage, page 89; Happy retirement, page 95; Thank you, page 86; Key to the door, page 93; Confirmation, page 96; Good luck, page 91. Tags and place settings can be found on page 97.

Thank you

Whatever the reason, there can be no nicer way to send thanks than with this pretty floral bouquet

❖ Ivory linen, 28 count 13 x 10.5cm (5¹⁄₈in x 4¹⁄₈in)
❖ DMC stranded cotton (floss) as listed in the key
❖ Tapestry needle, No 26
❖ Peach card with a 9.5 x 7.2cm (3³⁄₄ x 2⁷⁄₈in) rectangular opening
❖ Cream lace
❖ Blue flower-shaped beads

DESIGN SIZE: 8.6 x 6.8cm (3³⁄₈ x 2⁵⁄₈in)
NOTE: each stitch on the chart is worked over two threads of linen. Glue cream lace around the opening cut in the card, with a flower-shaped bead in each corner. A matching tag can be found on page 97.

Thank you designed by Anne Wilson

Thank you

DMC stranded cotton (floss)

	Xst	BS	FK
309			
554	U		
701	S		
703	▽		
725	O		
726	×		
800	<		
956	=		
957	↑		
3340	→		
3776	I		

Driving test

It's a great feeling to pass that test! Send your congratulations with this super card

❖ White Aida, 14 count 11 x 12.5cm (4⅜ x 5in)
❖ DMC stranded cotton (floss) as listed in the key
❖ Tapestry needle, No 24
❖ Blue card – no opening

DESIGN SIZE: 7 x 8.5cm (2¾ x 3⅜in)
NOTE: the lettering is backstitched using two strands of stranded cotton (floss). Fray the edges of the fabric by removing two rows of Aida on all sides of the design. Use double sided tape to attach the stitching to the front of the card.

Driving Test designed by Maria Diaz

Driving test			
DMC stranded cotton (floss)			
	Xst	BS	FK
Blanc	⊡		
310	■	⧄	
322	▨	⧄	
334	◘		
666	▥		
741	⊠		
762	→		
828	H		
3325	U		

Special friend

Whatever the occasion, these pretty violets will convey your love and best wishes

- ❖ Pale yellow evenweave, 28 count 12.5 x 10cm (5 x 4in)
- ❖ DMC stranded cotton (floss) as listed in the key
- ❖ Tapestry needle, No 26
- ❖ Mauve card with a 7.3 x 7.3cm (2⅞ x 2⅞in) square opening

DESIGN SIZE: 7 x 6.75cm (2¾ x 2⅝in)
NOTE: each stitch on the chart is worked over two threads of evenweave.

Special friend designed by Anne Wilson

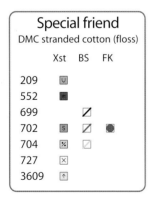

Special friend

DMC stranded cotton (floss)

	Xst	BS	FK
209	U		
552	▦		
699		╱	
702	S	╱	◉
704	⅔	╱	
727	✕		
3609	↑		

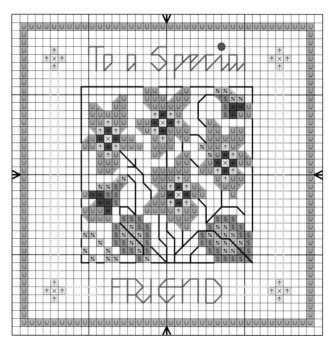

Bon voyage

Holiday or long journey, this stylized ocean liner is just right to send your best wishes

❖ Cream linen, 28 count 11 x 15cm (4⅝ x 6in)
❖ DMC stranded cotton (floss) as listed in the key
❖ Tapestry needle, No 26
❖ Beige card with a 8 x 10.5cm (3⅛ x 4⅛in) oval opening

DESIGN SIZE: 6 x 8cm (2⅜ x 3⅛in)
NOTE: each stitch on the chart is worked over two threads of evenweave fabric. A matching tag can be found on page 97.

Bon voyage designed by Claire Crompton

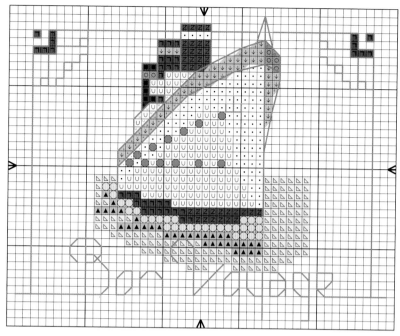

Bon voyage
DMC stranded cotton (floss)

	Xst	BS	FK
Blanc	·		
304			
347			
420		/	
451	⊙		
452	↓		
816			
827	◿		
3755	▲		
3866	U		

Congratulations

Exams at work, exams at school – these cards are ideal to send to the successful student of any age

❖ Cream evenweave, 28 count 15 x 11cm (6 x 4³⁄₈in)
❖ DMC stranded cotton (floss) as listed in the key
❖ Tapestry needle, No 26
❖ Blue card with a 8cm (3¹⁄₈in) diameter
   circular opening

DESIGN SIZE: 8 x 6.25cm (3¹⁄₈ x 2¹⁄₂in)
NOTE: each stitch on the card is worked over two threads of evenweave.

Congratulations designed by Mari Richards

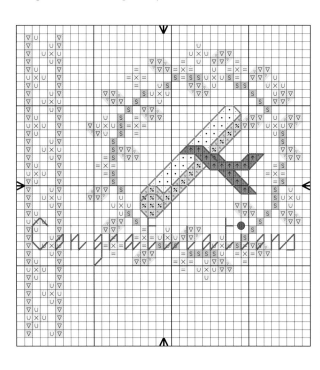

Congratulations
DMC stranded cotton (floss)

	Xst	BS	FK		Xst	BS	FK
Blanc	·			824		◪	●
414		◪		826	↑		
415	⅍			827	=		
727	✕			3816	S		
818	U			3817	▽		

You've passed

❖ Cream Aida, 14 count 9 x 11cm
   (3¹⁄₂ x 4³⁄₈in)
❖ DMC stranded cotton (floss) as listed
   in the key
❖ Gold metallic thread
❖ Tapestry needle, No 24
❖ Red card with a 6 x 8cm (2¹⁄₄ x 3¹⁄₈in)
   rectangular opening

DESIGN SIZE: 5.2 x 6.5cm (2 x 2¹⁄₂in)
NOTE: you've passed can be seen stitched
on page 6.

You've passed designed by Claire Crompton

You've passed
DMC stranded cotton (floss)

	Xst	BS	FK
304	■		
311	■		
322	N		
414	◉		
415	–		
420		◪	
422	U		▦
677	+		
895	■	◪	
Gold*	↑		

*DMC divisible gold
metallic thread

Good luck

Black cats, heather, clover leaves and horseshoes are all symbols of good luck, so here is a card with all four!

❖ White evenweave, 28 count 14 x 12cm
  (5½ x 4¾in)
❖ DMC stranded cotton (floss) as listed in the key
❖ Gold metallic thread
❖ Tapestry needle, No 26
❖ Gold card with a 9 x 7cm (3½ x 2¾in)
  rectangular opening
❖ Green paper

DESIGN SIZE: 8.2 x 6.5cm (3¼ x 2½in)
NOTE: each stitch on the chart is worked over two threads of evenweave. Cut four clover leaves and a stem from green paper using the shapes on page 110 as a guide. Glue them to the front of the card. A matching tag can be found on page 97.

Good luck designed by Lesley Teare

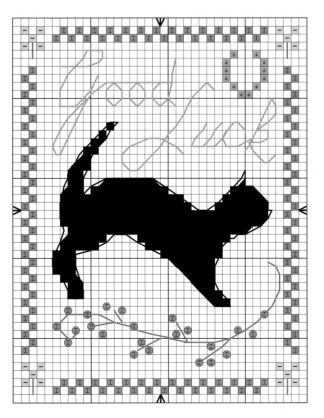

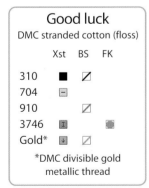

Good luck
DMC stranded cotton (floss)

	Xst	BS	FK
310	■	◪	
704	−		
910		◪	
3746	▣		◉
Gold*	▣	◪	

*DMC divisible gold
metallic thread

New job – Moving away

Send your best wishes to a friend or colleague who is changing jobs or moving away

❖ Cream Aida, 14 count 10.5 x 15cm (4⅛ x 6in)
❖ DMC stranded cotton (floss) as listed in the key
❖ Tapestry needle, No 24
❖ Blue card with a 8 x 10.5cm (3⅛ x 4⅛in) oval opening

DESIGN SIZE: 5 x 6.25cm (2 x 2½in)
NOTE: use two strands of stranded cotton (floss) for the backstitch lettering.

Moving away designed by Maria Diaz

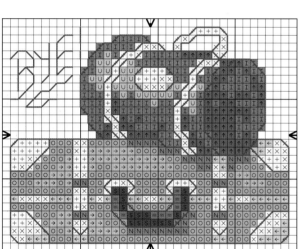

Moving away
DMC stranded cotton (floss)

	Xst	BS	FK
322	↑		
334	I		
435	N		
436	O		
437	→		
644	←		
712	+		
822	×		
931	⊞		
3325	U		
3750	S	╱	

New hat

❖ Pale blue Aida, 14 count 15 x 10.2cm (6 x 4in)
❖ DMC stranded cotton (floss) as listed in the key
❖ Tapestry needle, No 24
❖ Gold metallic thread
❖ Grey card with a 7.5 x 5.7cm (3 x 2¼in) rectangular opening
❖ Gold metallic pen

DESIGN SIZE: 7 x 4.8cm (2¾ x 1⅞in)
NOTE: use two strands of gold metallic thread to backstitch the hat. Draw a gold line using the metallic pen around the opening cut in the card. New hat can be seen stitched on page 6.

New hat designed by Claire Crompton

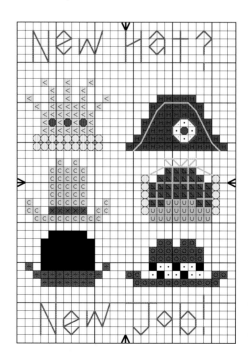

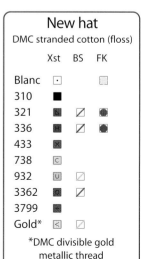

New hat
DMC stranded cotton (floss)

	Xst	BS	FK
Blanc	·		▨
310	■		
321	▩	╱	●
336	H	╱	●
433	▨		
738	C		
932	U	╱	
3362	▨	╱	
3799	▨		
Gold*	<	╱	

*DMC divisible gold metallic thread

New home – Little house

Moving house can be stressful as well as exciting, so bring a little sunshine with these pretty cards

❖ Ecru Aida, 14 count 8 x 6.75cm (3⅛ x 2⅝in)
❖ DMC stranded cotton (floss) as listed in the key
❖ Tapestry needle, No 24
❖ Cream card – no opening
❖ Brown handmade paper

DESIGN SIZE: 6.75 x 5.25cm (2⅝ x 2⅛in)
NOTE: fray the edges of the stitching by removing two rows of Aida around the design. Use double sided tape to attach first the handmade paper, then the stitching to the front of the card.

Little house designed by Sue Cook

Little house
DMC stranded cotton (floss)

	Xst	BS	FK		Xst	BS	FK
Blanc	·			991	▣		
153	–			993	↑		
155	◥			3761	◪		
351	S			3854	+		
727	=			3855	◤		
838	■		◹				

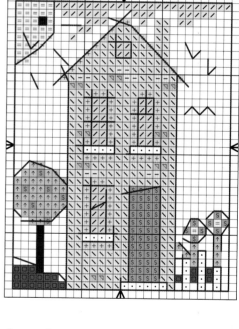

Key to the door
DMC stranded cotton (floss)

	Xst	BS	FK
Blanc	·		
157	⊠		
161	U		
676	▤		
725	↑		
727	⅔		
733	▽		
746	S		
838			◹
921	➡		
922	I		
3328	◪		
3820	H		

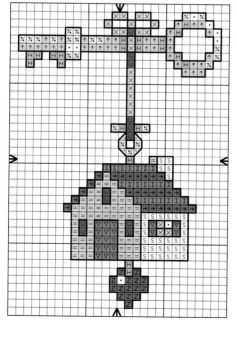

Key to the door

❖ Ecru Aida, 14 count 11.5 x 9cm (4½ x 3½in)
❖ DMC stranded cotton (floss) as listed in the key
❖ Tapestry needle, No 24
❖ Pale blue card with a 8 x 5.5cm (3⅛ x 2¼in) rectangular opening

DESIGN SIZE: 7 x 5cm (2¾ x 2in)
NOTE: key to the door can be seen stitched on page 85. A matching tag can be found on page 97.

Key to the door designed by Sue Cook

Get well soon – Briar rose

'An apple a day keeps the doctor away', but if it doesn't then these cards are sure to make the patient feel better

- Antique white evenweave, 30 count 11.5 x 9cm (4½ x 3½in)
- DMC stranded cotton (floss) as listed in the key
- Tapestry needle, No 26
- Cream card with a 8 x 5.5cm (3⅛ x 2¼in) arch shaped opening

Design Size: 6.75 x 4.5cm (2⅝ x 1¾in)
Note: each stitch on the chart is worked over two threads of fabric. Use the trace on page 110 to cut an arch shape in the front of the card

Briar rose designed by Lesley Teare

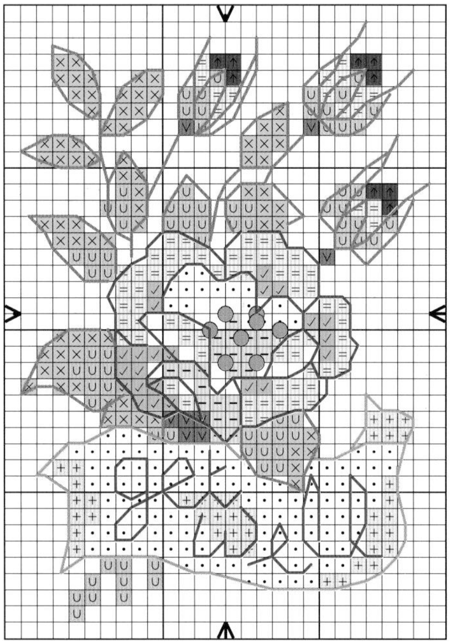

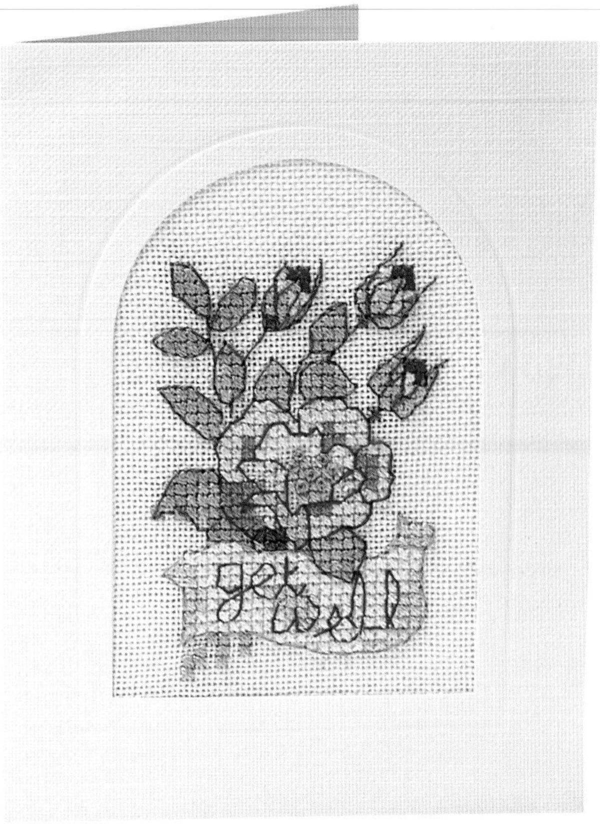

Briar rose
DMC stranded cotton (floss)

	Xst	BS	FK
326	↑	✓	
704	×		
776	−		
899	✓		
905	V	✓	
3047	+		
3348	U		
3713	=		
3823	·		
3852		✓	✓

Apple a day

- Ecru Aida, 14 count 14.5 x 11cm (5¾ x 4⅜in)
- DMC stranded cotton (floss) as listed in the key
- Tapestry needle, No 24
- Sage green card with a 8.5 x 7.5cm (3⅜ x 3in) heart shaped opening

Design Size: 5 x 6.25cm (2 x 2½in)
Note: use two strands of stranded cotton (floss) for the backstitch. Use the trace on page 109 to cut a heart shape in the front of the card. Apple a day can be seen stitched on page 6.

Apple a day designed by Claire Crompton

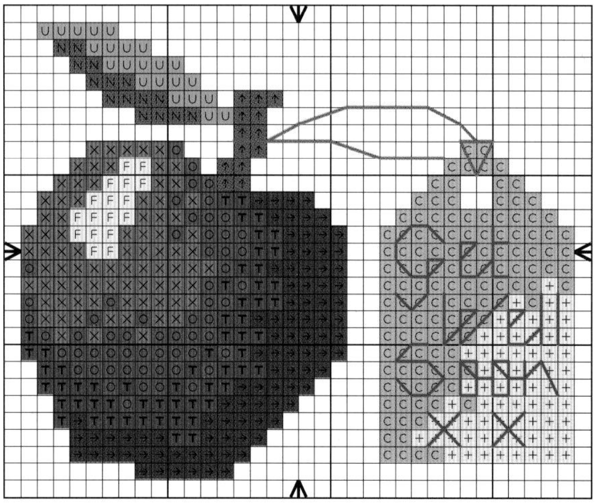

Apple a day
DMC stranded cotton (floss)

	Xst	BS	FK		Xst	BS	FK
336		✓		815	→		
498	T			3328	×		
543	+			3831	O		
561	N			3864	C		
562	U			3865	F		
779	↑	✓					

Retirement

If you know someone who is retiring, then this bright cheerful card is just right to wish them all the best

❖ White evenweave, 28 count 11 x 13.5cm (4³/₈ x 5¹/₄in)
❖ DMC stranded cotton (floss) as listed in the key
❖ Tapestry needle, No 26
❖ Blue card with a 7.5 x 9cm (3 x 3¹/₂in) rectangular opening

DESIGN SIZE: 7 x 8.5cm (2³/₄ x 3³/₈in)
NOTE: each stitch on the chart is worked over two threads of evenweave. A matching tag can be found on page 97.

Retirement designed by Anne Wilson

Retirement
DMC stranded cotton (floss)

	Xst	BS	FK
368	⊠		
561	▦	◩	
725	↑		
729	I	◩	
761	%		
892	§	◩	⊕
996	→		
3706	▽		

Confirmation

Being confirmed is a very important step in a Christian's life, so this card is a wonderful keepsake of that special day

❖ White linen, 28 count 11 x 15cm (4⅜ x 6in)
❖ DMC stranded cotton (floss) as listed in the key
❖ Tapestry needle, No 26
❖ White card with a 7 x 9cm (2¾ x 3½in) rectangular opening

DESIGN SIZE: 6.3 x 8.2cm (2½ x 3¼in)
NOTE: each stitch on the chart is worked over two threads of linen. Use the alphabet and numbers on page 98 to add a name and date to the card. A matching tag can be found on page 97.

Confirmation designed by Helen Philipps

Confirmation
DMC stranded cotton (floss)

	Xst	BS	FK
436	U		
840		✓	
841	✕	✓	
3033	↑		

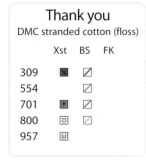

Thank you
DMC stranded cotton (floss)

	Xst	BS	FK
309	▨	▨	
554		▨	
701	▲	▨	
800	◙	▨	
957	⊍		

The thank you tag can be seen stitched with its matching card on page 85. The card chart can be found on page 86. Designed by Anne Wilson.

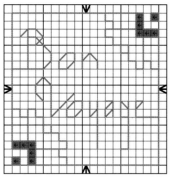

Bon voyage
DMC stranded cotton (floss)

	Xst	BS	FK
304	▣		
420		▨	

The bon voyage tag can be seen stitched with its matching card on page 84. The card chart can be found on page 89. Designed by Claire Crompton.

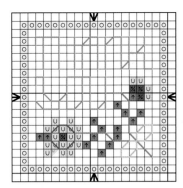

Good luck
DMC stranded cotton (floss)

	Xst	BS	FK
310	■	▨	
704	▭		
910	▨		

The good luck tag can be seen stitched with its matching card on page 84. Use the trace on page 110 to cut a flower shape from green card. The card chart can be found on page 91. Designed by Lesley Teare.

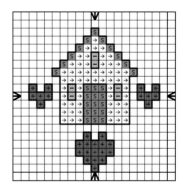

Turn to the matching card chart pages for details of the fabric used in making these tags. General finishing instructions can be found on page 102.

Key to the door
DMC stranded cotton (floss)

	Xst	BS	FK
157	▭		
161	▪		
746	▣		
838		▨	
3328	⊞		

The key to the door tag can be seen stitched with its matching card on page 85. The card chart can be found on page 93. Designed by Sue Cook.

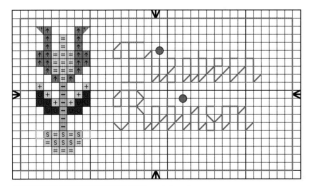

Happy retirement
DMC stranded cotton (floss)

	Xst	BS	FK
368	⊞		
561	■		
725	▤		
729	▭	▨	
892	▲	▨	◉
996	▪		

The happy retirement place setting can be seen stitched with its matching card on page 84. The card chart can be found on page 95, and the alphabet on page 98. Designed by Anne Wilson.

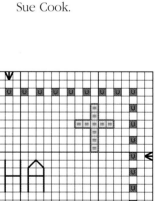

Confirmation
DMC stranded cotton (floss)

	Xst	BS	FK
436	⊞		
840		▨	
841	⊍	▨	
3033	▤		

The Confirmation place setting can be seen stitched with its matching card on page 84. The card chart can be found on page 96, and the alphabet on page 98. Designed by Helen Philipps.

Alphabets and Numbers

Use the alphabets and numbers on the next four pages to personalize the cards and tags in this book. A page reference for where each has been used is indicated on the charts

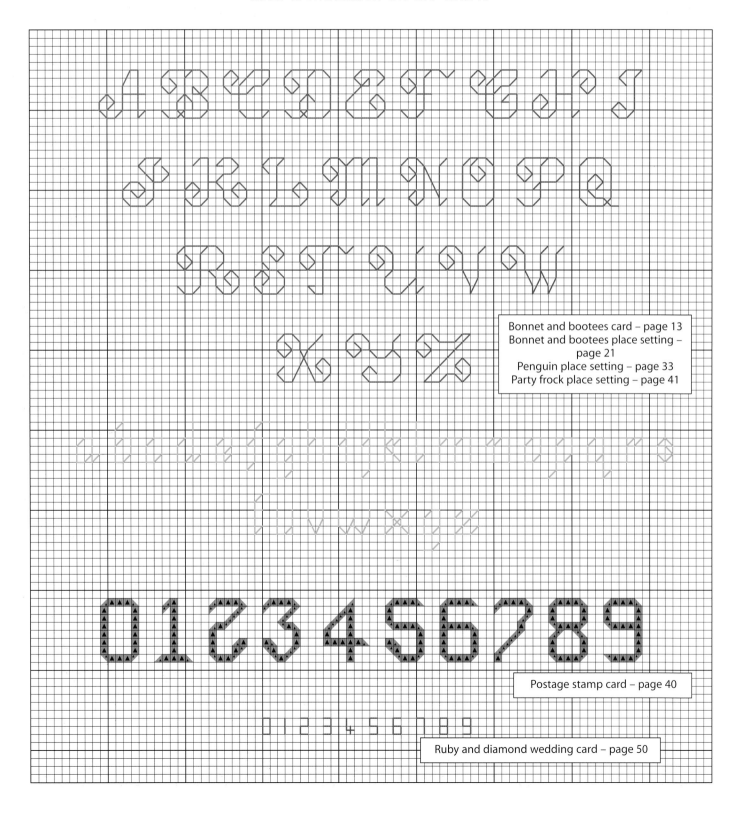

Bonnet and bootees card – page 13
Bonnet and bootees place setting –
page 21
Penguin place setting – page 33
Party frock place setting – page 41

Postage stamp card – page 40

Ruby and diamond wedding card – page 50

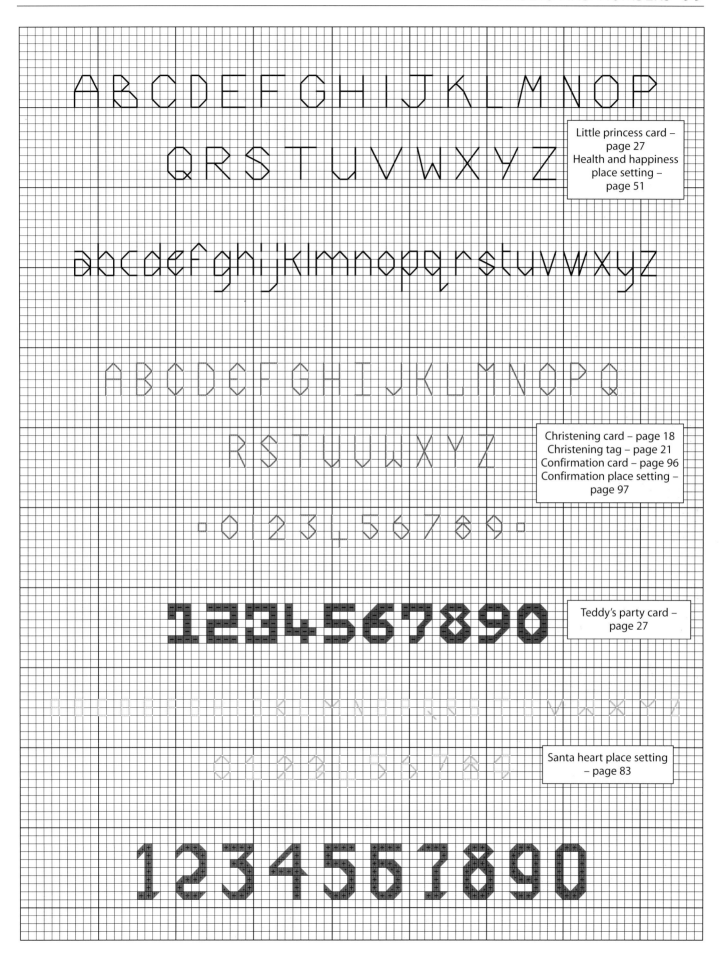

Little princess card –
page 27
Health and happiness
place setting –
page 51

Christening card – page 18
Christening tag – page 21
Confirmation card – page 96
Confirmation place setting –
page 97

Teddy's party card –
page 27

Santa heart place setting
– page 83

123456789

Racing car card –
page 24

ABCDEFGHIJKL

MNOPQRST

UVWXYZ

Happy retirement place
setting – page 97

abcdefghijklmno

pqrstuvwxyz

1234567890

Anniversary cake
card – page 48

1234567890   TH ST RD

Spaceship card –
page 24

1234567890

abcdefghijklmnopqrst
uvwxyz

Daisy card – page 25
New Year place
setting – page 65

ABCDEFGHIJKLMNOPQ
RSTUVWXYZ

Out to play card – page 26
Out to play tag – page 41
Swans place setting – page 51

ABCDEFGHIJ
KLMNOPQ
RSTUVWXYZ

ABCDEFGHIJKLMNOPQR
STUVWXYZ

1234567890

Mounting and Finishing

Once your stitching has been completed you will be ready to mount it into a card. Card mounts are available in an enormous variety of colours, shapes and sizes. On the next few pages you will find instructions for decorating card mounts with gold lines, paper shapes, jewels and ribbon. If you have trouble finding a mount to fit your design, or you need an unusual shape or colour, then it is very easy to create your own. Most art supplies shops carry a good range of coloured card, and with very little equipment – just a scalpel, craft mat and ruler – you will soon be creating original mounts for your stitching.

A selection of craft material that can be used to create interesting card mounts. Making cards and tags can be found on page 104; mounting your stitching on page 105; and decorating card mounts on page 106.

Making cards and tags

Small designs look wonderful when mounted in greetings cards and are guaranteed to bring pleasure to the recipient. Mounts can be bought ready-made, or cut from thin card and then decorated to complement the stitching.

Cutting cards and tags

Ready-made card mounts are available from needlecraft shops in a wide range of colours, shapes and sizes, but if you are looking for an unusual shape then it is easy to cut your own from thin card using a scalpel and ruler. Cards and tags can be double-folded (three panels) with a shaped opening, so that the stitching is attached to the back of the middle section, and the card stands on one flap; single-folded (two panels) with no opening, so that the stitching is attached to the front of the card, and the card stands on the back flap; and single sheet tags, where the stitching is attached to the front, and the tag has a ribbon or string tie through one corner.

1 A double-folded card has three panels and two score lines. Using a pencil, straight edge and craft knife, mark then cut a rectangle the height, and three times the width of the card. The corners must be exact right angles or the edges will not come together when folded. If you are making a single-folded card, cut two panels, leaving out flap (c), and make one score line down the centre.

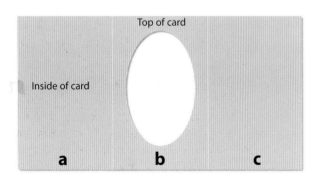

A double-folded card is divided into three equal sections (see diagram above):
(a) folds over on to (b) and covers the back of the stitching.
(b) has an aperture, and is where the stitching is attached.
(c) is the flap that is used to stand the card up.

2 Draw two fine pencil lines down the front of the card to divide it into three. So that the card fits together neatly, cut 1mm (1/16in) from the left edge of panel (a), which will make it slightly narrower than the other two. Score the two vertical pencil lines using the back of the craft knife blade. This will make a sharp indentation, but will not cut the card.

3 With the scored lines on the outside, fold the card twice, making the slightly smaller flap (a) fold in first to cover the back of the stitching. Run your thumb nail down the folds to make a well defined crease.

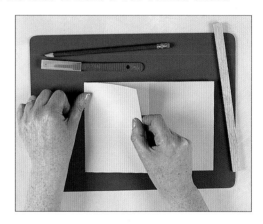

4 Make a paper template of the opening to be cut in the card. Lay the template on the front middle section (b) of the card, and draw around it with a pencil. For simpler shapes use a ruler and pencil, or a compass.

5 Place the card flat on a craft mat, with the pencil lines uppermost. Use a scalpel to cut slowly following the pencil lines, making sure you cut back exactly to the point where you started.

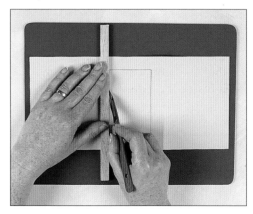

6 Remove the cut out section from the card flap (b). Use the blunt end of the scalpel to rub around the edges of the opening, this will burnish the cut and remove any rough edges. Your card is now ready for mounting your stitching.

Mounting cards and tags

It is important that before you start assembling the card you identify the top of the card mount, the left flap that will cover the back of the stitching, and the flap that will prop up the card. To do this, look at the diagram on the opposite page: when the card mount is face down on the table, the top of the card will have a smaller border around the aperture than at the bottom, and the left flap (a) will be used to cover the back of the stitching.

You will need for mounting cards:

❖ Your stitching
❖ Craft mat
❖ Pins
❖ Scissors
❖ Card mount
❖ Double-sided tape
❖ White paper
❖ Iron and soft cloth
❖ Scalpel, ruler and pencil for cutting the mount

1 Wash then press your stitching following the instructions on page 108. Lay the design face up on a craft mat and position the card over the design, so that the stitching is exactly in the middle of the card opening. Mark the corners of the card opening with pins.

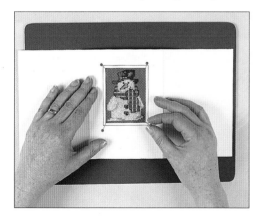

2 Leaving the pins and the fabric in place, carefully remove the card mount and then trim the fabric so that it will fit inside the card when folded up.

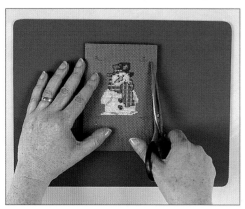

3 Turn the card over and stick a piece of white paper to the left-hand flap. Stick double-sided tape around the opening and peel off the backing tape.

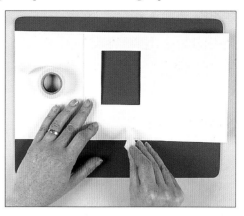

4 Use the pins to guide the card back into position, taking care not to touch the tape on any part of the card. Remove the pins, turn the card over and stick the left-hand flap (a) over the back of the stitching, pressing it well down on to the tape.

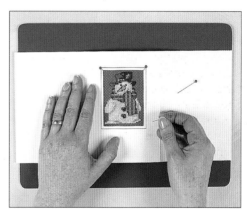

5 Fraying the fabric and attaching it to the front of a piece of card is a quick way to make a tag. Cut the fabric slightly larger than the stitching, leaving enough around the design to fray the edges. Cut a piece of card just larger than the fabric. Fray the edges of the design by removing several rows of fabric. Attach the stitching to the front of a tag with double-sided tape.

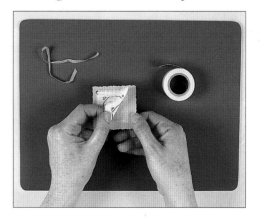

Decorating card mounts

Handmade paper, ribbon, beads and coloured paper stars are just a few of the many things that can be stuck to the surface of cards and tags for decoration. Almost any small item can be attached to the mount, as long as you remember that you will need to get the card into the envelope to post it. The easiest way to brighten a plain mount is to outline the opening cut in the card with a line drawn in metallic pen. As well as decorating the surface of the card mount, deckle-edged scissors can also be used to give the edges of the card added interest.

Outlining the aperture

One of the simplest ways to decorate a plain mount is by drawing a line around the opening cut in the card. Use a metallic pen with a fine nib; shake the pen well, and then make a straight, dotted or dashed line around the opening. On a circular opening you may prefer to draw freehand, but if your hand is unsteady, draw a pencil line around the opening, then work over it with the pen. On square or rectangular openings, use a ruler to draw a pencil line before going over it with a pen.

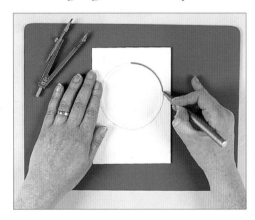

Cutting paper shapes

A paper shape can be used to fill a large area of blank card mount. Draw an interesting shape on white paper, then cut out the shape. Lay the shape on coloured paper or card, draw around the edges and then cut out. Attach the shape to the card mount using glue. A selection of small shapes can be found on pages 109-110.

Handmade paper decoration

Handmade paper can lift a simple card and turn it into something really special. Rough textured paper is best torn when slightly wet, and working against a ruler. Attach the paper to the mount using double-sided tape.

Ribbon trim

Ribbon is an attractive way to finish card mounts and can be used in many different ways. Always press the ribbon before you start to work, and use double-sided tape or fabric glue to attach it to the card.

Edge finishing

Deckle-edged scissors can be used on a mount to create an interesting finish. Draw a pencil line just in from the edge of the card. Cut slowly with the deckle-edged scissors, in long strokes, following the pencil line.

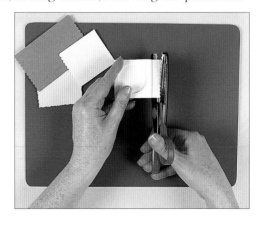

Stitching techniques

Most of the cards and tags in this book are simple to stitch – a combination of cross stitch, backstitch, french knots and beads. Below you will find working instructions for the stitches, and useful information on reading the charts

General stitching instructions

All the designs use two strands of stranded cotton (floss) for the cross stitch and three-quarter stitches, and one strand for the backstitch and french knots. If this is not the case the variation will be noted on each chart page.

Reading the charts

The charts are in colour, with a symbol printed in each square. Each square on the chart represents one cross stitch. In some cases, when working on finer fabric, each square on the chart is worked over two threads of fabric, if this is the case instructions will be given with the chart. All the charts have a key listing the DMC stranded cotton (floss) colours used in number order. The key also shows if there is backstitch, french knots or beads; the french knots and beads are shown as coloured dots on the key and chart. The beads are DMC and have been chosen to match the stranded cotton (floss) colours (more details on beads can be found in *Working with beads* on the next page). If you would prefer not to use beads then french knots can be used in their place. Most designs have a combination of whole cross stitch, three-quarter stitch and backstitch. The three-quarter stitches are shown on the chart as triangles of colour printed in the corners of a square. As well as a chart and key, each design has a list of materials, instructions and a design size.

Understanding the charts

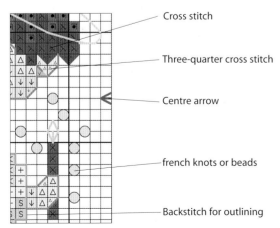

- Cross stitch
- Three-quarter cross stitch
- Centre arrow
- french knots or beads
- Backstitch for outlining

A section of chart showing the stitches used on the designs in this book: cross stitch, three-quarter stitch, backstitch, french knots and beads.

Fabric

The designs in this book are worked on Aida or evenweave fabric like linen. All the fabrics used for cross stitch should have the same number of horizontal and vertical threads to the inch. Aida has threads grouped together in blocks, so that one stitch is made over one block of threads using the holes as a guide. When working on the finer evenweave, like 36 count, the instructions may tell you to make each stitch over two or even four threads of fabric. A project sewn over two threads on 28 count fabric, for example, would come out the same size as if you stitched it on 14 count Aida. The fabric listed in the key shows the count, the colour, and the actual size of fabric needed for the design. When buying the fabric allow extra at the edges if you are intending to work the design in a hoop or small frame. If you want to stitch on a different count of fabric than shown on the project, you will have to calculate the finished size of the stitching before you buy the fabric. To do this, count the number of squares both high and wide of your chosen design – this is the stitch count. Then divide the two measurements by the number of threads per inch of your fabric. When you are stitching over two threads remember to divide the stitch count by half the number of threads per inch.

Needle and thread

Use a needle for cross stitch that is blunt and slips easily through the fabric without piercing it. A size 24 tapestry needle works best on 14 count Aida, while a 26 tapestry needle is best for finer fabric. A 26 tapestry needle should easily pass through the eye of most beads, but you may find that using a fine sewing needle is easier on some designs. All the designs in this book are stitched with DMC stranded cotton. Unless mentioned in the instructions given with each design, two strands should be used for the cross stitch, and one for the backstitch and french knots. If DMC metallic thread has been included in the design, use two strands for the cross stitch, unless a different number of strands has been given in the instructions. On a few designs two different stranded cotton (floss) colours have been blended together in the needle, in most cases one strand of each colour should be used. Where Kreinek blending filament is used on a design, a single strand should be added to the needle with the stranded cotton (floss) colour.

Preparing to stitch

Cut your fabric several inches larger than the size given in the project materials list. Zig-zag around the edges of the fabric or bind it with masking tape to prevent the edges fraying. Fold the fabric in four to find the centre point, and mark it with a pin or small stitch. Find the centre of the chart by following the arrows from the edges to the centre – this is where you begin stitching. Thread your needle and make a knot at one end of the thread. Push the needle to the back of the fabric about 3cm (1¼in) from your starting point, leaving the knot on the right side. Stitch towards the knot, securing the thread on the back of the fabric. When the thread is secure, cut off the knot. Finish the thread by weaving it through the back of the stitches.

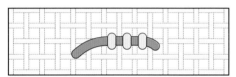

Hoop or frame

Most small designs can easily be stitched without mounting the fabric in a hoop or frame. If you do decide to use one, you will need to cut a larger piece of fabric than given in the materials list. Once the stitching has been completed the excess fabric can be cut away. Your project should always be removed from the hoop when you have finished stitching, to prevent a ring mark forming on the fabric.

Working with beads

The beads are shown on the charts and keys as coloured dots. For more details on understanding the charts and keys see *Reading the charts*, at the beginning of this chapter. All the beads used in this book match DMC stranded cotton (floss) colours. There are four different type of beads used: V1 general seed beads, V2 nostalgia, V3 metallic and V4 frosted. As well as the bead type, a colour code and colour description will also be listed. The beads should be attached to the stitching using two strands of stranded cotton (floss). Thread the bead on to the needle as you make the first part of the cross, then as you make the second part, lay one thread of stranded cotton (floss) either side of the bead, before pushing the needle back into the fabric and continuing.

Washing and pressing

Always wash your work before you mount it in a card or tag. To do this, swish the stitching in luke warm water and, if the colours bleed, rinse in fresh water until the water is clear. Do not be tempted to stop rinsing unless you are absolutely sure the bleeding has stopped. Roll the stitching in a clean towel and squeeze gently to remove most of the water. On a second towel, place your design face down, cover with a cloth and iron until dry.

Working the stitches

Cross stitch Each coloured square on the chart represents one cross stitch on the fabric. A cross stitch is worked in two stages: a diagonal stitch is worked over one block of Aida, or two threads of finer evenweave fabric like linen, from the bottom left of the stitch to the top right. The second part of the stitch is worked from bottom right to top left to form a cross. When working a block of stitches in the same colour, stitch a line of half crosses before completing each stitch on the return journey. Make sure that the top half of each cross lies in the same direction.

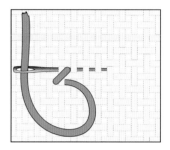

Three-quarter stitch Each stitch is shown on the chart as a coloured triangle. A three-quarter stitch is a half stitch (the first part of a cross stitch) with a quarter stitch worked from one of the remaining corners to the middle of the stitch. It is easier to work fractional stitches when each stitch is being worked over two threads of fabric (like linen or fine evenweave). When stitching on Aida you will have to pierce the middle of the fabric block with a sharp needle to make a hole for the quarter stitch.

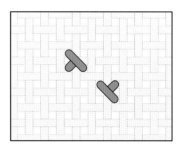

Backstitch This is shown on the chart as a solid coloured line, and may be used on the chart in several different ways: as an outline to give definition to an area of stitches; on top of the cross stitch to give detail; on its own, to create areas of lettering or detail lines. Backstitch can be worked as single stitches over one or two threads of fabric, or as longer stitches to cover a larger area.

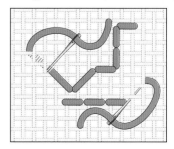

Use the templates on these pages to create and decorate your own card mounts.

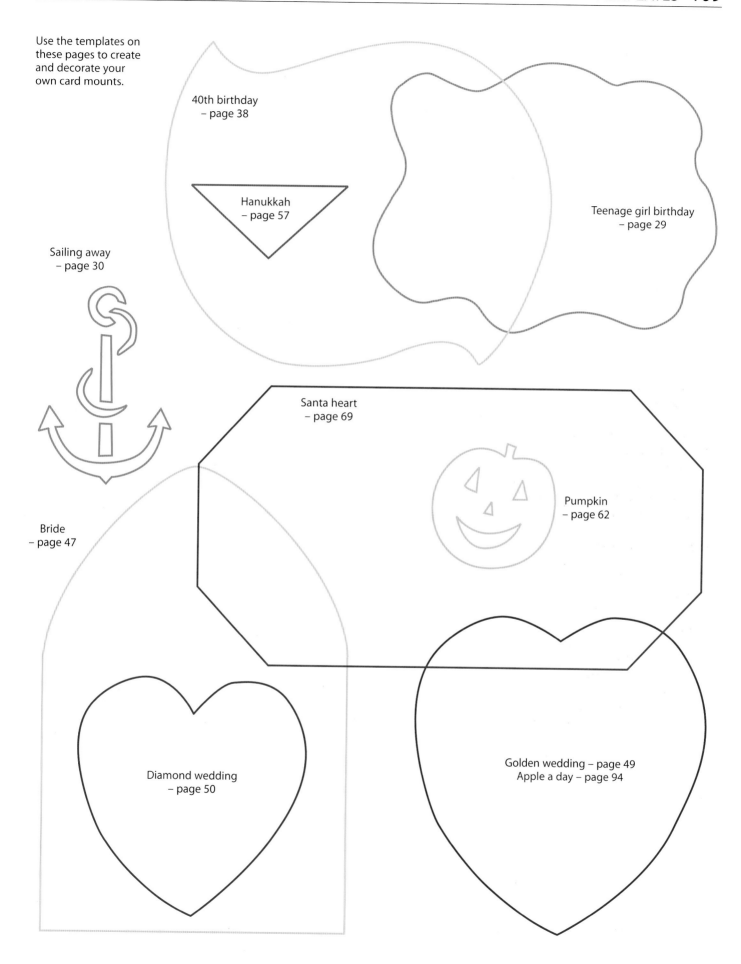

40th birthday
– page 38

Hanukkah
– page 57

Teenage girl birthday
– page 29

Sailing away
– page 30

Santa heart
– page 69

Pumpkin
– page 62

Bride
– page 47

Diamond wedding
– page 50

Golden wedding – page 49
Apple a day – page 94

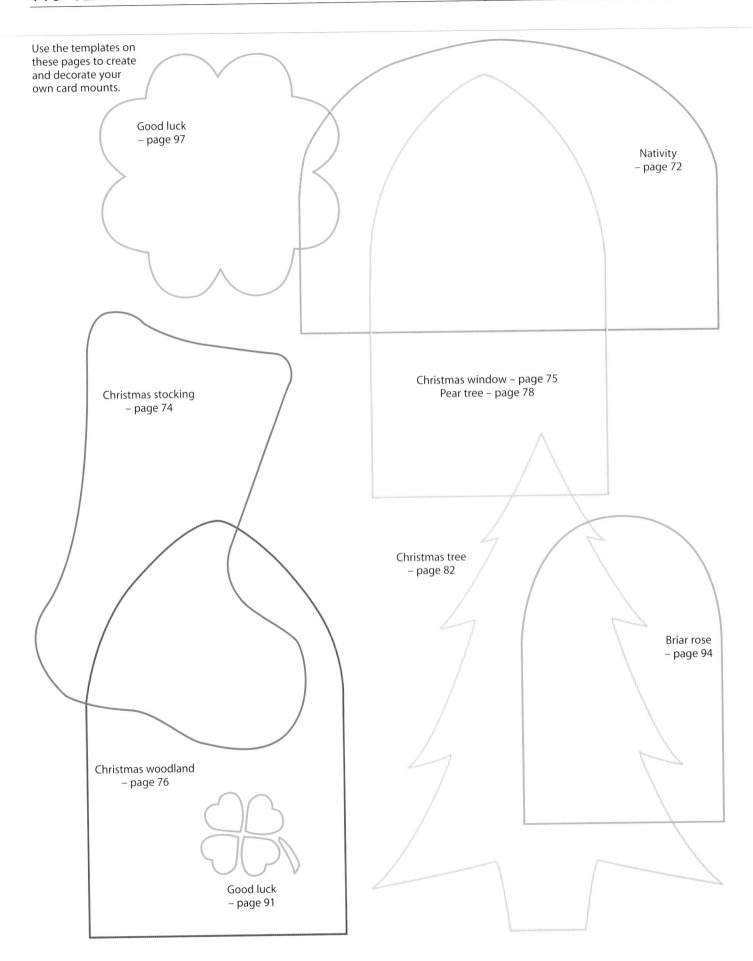

Use the templates on these pages to create and decorate your own card mounts.

Good luck
– page 97

Nativity
– page 72

Christmas stocking
– page 74

Christmas window – page 75
Pear tree – page 78

Christmas tree
– page 82

Briar rose
– page 94

Christmas woodland
– page 76

Good luck
– page 91

Acknowledgements

The publishers would like to thank the following people: Sue Cook, Julie Cook, Claire Crompton, Maria Diaz, Sam Hawkins, Susan Penny, Helen Philipps, Mari Richards, Lesley Teare, Anne Wilson for their design contributions; Michaela Learner for her expert stitching; Doreen Holland for her chart checking; and Susan and Martin Penny for producing the book.

The following designers can be contacted at the addresses below:
Sue Cook at The August Moon Design Company Limited, 32 Wavell Drive, Malpas, Newport, Gwent NP20 6QN. Website: www.augustmoon.co.uk.
Susan Penny at Penny & Penny, 135 Bay View Road, Northam, Devon EX39 1BJ. email: penny.andpenny@virgin.net
Helen Philipps at Merry Heart Designs, PO Box 110, Hoylake, Wirral CH48 2WD. Website: www.merryheart.co.uk.

Suppliers

When writing to any of the companies below, please include a stamped addressed envelope for your reply.

DMC Creative World Ltd
Pullman Road, Wigston, Leicester LE8 2DY
Zweigart Aida, linen and stranded cotton.

Coats Crafts Ltd
PO Box 22, The Lingfield Estate, McMullen Road,
Darlington, Co Durham DL1 1YQ
Kreinek blending filament.

Craft Creations Ltd
2C Ingersoll House, Dalamare Road, Cheshunt, Herts
EN8 9ND
Card mounts.

Impress Cards & Craft Materials
Slough Farm, Westhall, Halesworth, Suffolk
IP19 8RN
Card mounts.

The DMC Corporation
Port Kearney Bld, 10 South Kearney,
NJ 070732-0650, USA
Zweigart Aida, linen and stranded cotton.

Gay Bowles Sales Inc
PO Box 1060, Janesville, WI, USA

Anne Brinkley Designs Inc
761 Palmer Avenue, Holmdel, NJ 97733, USA

Ireland Needlecraft Pty Ltd
2-4 Keppel Drive, Hallam, Victoria 3803, Australia

DMC Needlecraft Pty
PO Box 317, Earlswood 2206, New South Wales
2204, Australia
Zweigart Aida, linen and stranded cotton.

Index

An entry in *italics* indicates where an illustration does not appear on its project page. **Bold** indicates a matching tag.